SAVING THE BEAST

A recovering reporter reflects on America's broken media and how to fix it

TED CZECH

Copyright © 2024 Ted Czech

All Rights Reserved

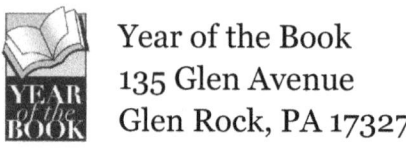
Year of the Book
135 Glen Avenue
Glen Rock, PA 17327

978-1-64649-408-8 (paperback)

978-1-64649-409-5 (ebook)

Cover art CoPilot Designer
Cover design PixelStudio

No part of this publication may be reproduced, distributed, or transmitted in any form or by any means, including photocopying, recording, or other electronic or mechanical methods, without the prior written permission of the publisher, except in the case of brief quotations embodied in critical reviews and certain other noncommercial uses permitted by copyright law.

Dedication

I dedicate this book to my parents, Ted and Betty Ann Czech, who gave me life, gave me my creativity, and supported me in all my endeavors, hairbrained and otherwise.

To Theresa M. "Nana" Nardis, my mother-in-law, who passed away in early 2024. I'm sorry I didn't get this done sooner so you could have seen it.

To my wife and our two sons, for your love and patience with all the hours I spent in "the study." You mean everything to me.

Contents

Special Bulletin – Trump Assassination Attempt 1
Introduction – The Day the News Died 5
PART I – DESTRUCTION
Chapter 1 – Decades of Deception 13
Chapter 2 – 24 Hours is Not Enough 25
Chapter 3 – The Disregard of Objectivity 33
Chapter 4 – The Rise of Reporter-activists 41
Chapter 5 – All-in on the Deception 47
Chapter 6 – Fact-checking Is Unnecessary 69
PART 2 – FALLOUT
Chapter 7 – Donald Trump.. 81
Chapter 8 – Elon Musk 89
Chapter 9 – Media Sows Distrust and Pays the Price 103
Chapter 10 – Land of Layoffs 109
Chapter 11 – Dreams Don't Pay the Bills 117
Chapter 12 – Tucker Carlson Out at Fox News 121
Chapter 13 – Reporters Fired for Social Media Vigilantism 127
Chapter 14 – The Dawn of Independent/Citizen Journalists 135
Chapter 15 – Local Ownership in News Deserts 151
PART 3 – RECKONING
Chapter 16 – The Other Way Doesn't Work................................ 161
Chapter 17 – Mea Culpas 165
Chapter 18 – Do the Work 171

Chapter 19 – More Whistleblowers 183

Chapter 20 - Teach Journalism the Right Way.............................189

Chapter 21 – Resist Focusing on Race... 191

Chapter 22 – No Donations..197

Chapter 23 – Continue Covering Local News 209

Chapter 24 – Cover Crime the Way It Should Be Covered.........213

Chapter 25 – Have Business People Run the Business of
    Newspapers 223

Chapter 26 – Get Rid of Personality-driven News 225

Chapter 27 – Let the Creativity Flow 229

Chapter 28 – Say Goodbye to AI 233

CONCLUSION – Now What? 245

SPECIAL BULLETIN – TRUMP ASSASSINATION ATTEMPT

Do you remember where you were when JFK was shot, or Ronald Reagan? How about the Challenger explosion or the terrorist attacks on Sept. 11? We now have a new landmark historical moment to add to that tragic tally – the attempted assassination of Republican Presidential nominee Donald J. Trump at 6:11 PM on July 13, 2024, in Butler, Pennsylvania.

Following the sniper attack on Trump, I had a decision to make – already past my deadline to finish this book, should I include an additional chapter about what happened? The decision was a swift and resounding yes, not only for the sheer magnitude of what occurred, but because of the media's sheer incompetence in reporting the incident.

A primary pestilence plaguing journalism today is that the thirst to be first usually means you are the worst. In journalism, you want to be timely in your reporting to inform the public, and in harnessing that speed, you will get more eyeballs on your product, because journalism is both a public service and a business. However, communicating the first nugget of information you receive, no matter how uncooked, is downright irresponsible. But yet, that's exactly what happened.

Here's a headline from the Associated Press Facebook page, posted at 6:23 PM, 12 minutes after the assassination attempt: "BREAKING: Donald Trump has been escorted off the stage by Secret Service during a rally after loud noises ring out in the crowd." Below a photo of a bloody but brazen Trump surrounded by Secret Service agents, was another line: "Donald Trump whisked off stage in Pennsylvania after loud noises rang through the crowd."

I clicked on the link more than a week later, to see the headline to the actual story had been amended: "Trump injured but 'fine' after attempted assassination at rally, shooter and one attendee are dead."[1]

In this case, the media, including the AP, desperately needed a giant syringe of two drugs – WAIT and CONFIRM. But that is the one thing journalists detest more than anything... waiting. It's beaten into plebes in J-school that if you wait, especially in reporting breaking news, you might miss a deadline, fail to reach that pivotal source, or arrive at the crime scene after everything is cleaned up.

But the AP, in its fool's errand to be first, went with "loud noises"? What were they, a nearby train's horn? Somebody banging pots and pans? A protester blasting an air horn? This sows confusion rather than provides clarity. The right thing to do would have been to wait and get an official word as quickly as possible.

Paul Fahri of *The Washington Post* said the media was cautious in their reporting and that because they waited, they were criticized.[2] I disagree. The media was taken behind the woodshed because they did not wait. Instead, they hastily blasted out the smallest morsels of sketchy information, most of it incorrect.

If CNN wanted to exercise discretion, they would not have written the headline, "Secret Service rushes Trump off stage after he falls at rally." Totally incomplete and misleading. He fell, as in he lost his balance? I bet they were just chomping at the bit to write that, after President Joe Biden's numerous falls during his presidency. *USAToday* described the gunshots as "loud noises," as did the *Chicago Tribune*, and NBC called them "popping noises." Instead of all this vague conjecture, simply report that Trump was rushed off stage by Secret Service, he appears to be bleeding from his ear, and we'll get further details as they become available.3

But the media doesn't worry about casting an incomplete headline to the public because they can just update it online like the first one never happened with a little "stealth editing."4

Then came the caterwauling pundits. At some point following the assassination attempt, the NBCUniversal bigwigs made the decision to have one feed on the assassination broadcasted on NBC, NBC News Now, and MSNBC. This drew the ire of MSNBC's Morning Joe hosts and married couple Joe Scarborough and Mika Brzezinski, who were told the day after the attempt not to show up Monday for work.5 In response, the couple threatened to leave their jobs the next time they were replaced by a feed.6

But there was apparently more to the story. According to CNN, "the decision was made to avoid a scenario in which one of the show's stable of two dozen-plus guests might make an inappropriate comment on live television that could be used to assail the program and network as a whole."7

But MSNBC refused to muzzle another of its personalities, Joy Reid. She preposterously suggested the assassination attempt was a "photo-op." She also stated that Biden surviving Covid was equal to Trump rising to his feet, blood streaming across his face, raising his fist and yelling, "Fight! Fight! Fight!" after nearly getting his head blown off.8 Yep, definitely the same thing. Trump could have allowed Secret Service agents to roll him out on a stretcher, but he refused, insisting he walk out as a show of strength.

I understand that political critics are expected to pontificate opinions, and we know what to expect on a liberal-leaning network such as MSNBC, but Scarborough, Brzezinski, and Reid appeared to be consumed with enmity, which has rendered them incapable of any sense of fairness or even common sense. Their only aim is the annihilation of a man – legally, politically, financially – even in possibly the most traumatic moment of Trump's life.

This is but one example of why I am writing this book. So read on, true believer.

---

[1] McMurray, Patty. "LIST OF TEN MOST Misleading Mainstream Media Headlines After Failed Trump Assassination." The Gateway Pundit, July 14, 2024. https://www.thegatewaypundit.com/2024/07/list-ten-most-dishonest-mainstream-media-headlines-after/.

[2] Farhi, Paul. "How the media's wait for the facts in Trump shooting fed a backlash." *The Washington Post*, July 15, 2024. https://www.washingtonpost.com/style/media/2024/07/15/media-backlash-trump-shooting/.

[3] Ibid.

[4] The Arweave Project. "What is stealth editing, and how can we combat it?" Medium.com, Dec. 6, 2018. https://arweave.medium.com/what-is-stealth-editing-and-how-can-we-combat-it-98052078b517.

[5] Linebarger, Cullen. "MSNBC Yanks Trump-Hating "Morning Joe" Off the Air Following Trump Assassination Attempt." The Gateway Pundit, July 15, 2024. https://www.thegatewaypundit.com/2024/07/msnbc-yanks-trump-hating-morning-joe-air-following/.

[6] Lynch, James. "Scarborough Threatens to Quit Morning Joe after MSNBC Cancels Episode in Wake of Trump Assassination Attempt." National Review, July 16, 2024. https://www.nationalreview.com/news/scarborough-threatens-to-quit-morning-joe-after-msnbc-cancels-episode-in-wake-of-trump-assassination-attempt/.

[7] Darcy, Oliver. "'Morning Joe' pulled from air Monday because of Trump shooting." CNN, July 15, 2024. https://www.cnn.com/2024/07/14/media/msnbc-morning-joe-pulled-trump-assassination/index.html.

[8] LaChance, Mike. "MSNBC's Joy Reid Suggests Biden Surviving COVID is the Same as Trump Surviving an Assassination Attempt (VIDEO)." The Gateway Pundit, July 17, 2024. https://www.thegatewaypundit.com/2024/07/msnbcs-joy-reid-suggests-biden-surviving-covid-is/

Introduction – The Day the News Died

Feed the beast.

It was both a newsroom battle cry and a lamentation of reporters on deadline. The beast – journalism – required nourishment, that is news, to be satiated.

Several decades ago, the beast survived organically, receiving sustenance through professionalism, fairness, and objectivity. But more recently, the ingredients have been tainted by parasites such as advocacy and solidarity journalism, and both-sides-ism.

The beast is dying.

The fresh ingredients mentioned above are tethered to the absolute bedrock of journalism – the First Amendment of the United States Constitution. It allows for freedom of speech and freedom of the press, but in the ultimate irony, it is now under attack by the very people expected to practice it.

On June 22, 2021, Katherine Maher, who at the time had left positions as CEO and executive director of the Wikimedia Foundation, had this to say about the First Amendment:

> "The First Amendment ... is a fairly robust protection of rights ... for platforms ... to be able to regulate what kind of content they want on their sites, but it also means that it is a little bit tricky to really address some of the real challenges of where does bad information come from and some of the influence peddlers who have made a real market economy around it."[1]

Wait a minute, hold on.

The First Amendment is "tricky" and a "challenge"? And what exactly does she mean by "bad information"?

Less than two years later, Maher would assume leadership of one of the most influential media outlets in America, National Public Radio.

There also seemed to be a case of cognitive dissonance when it came to feeding the beast. Emma Tucker, Chief Editor of the *Wall Street Journal*, was part of a panel discussion in January 2024 at the World Economic Forum's annual conference when she may have inadvertently pulled back the curtain. "If you go back really not that long ago, as I say, we owned the news," Tucker said. "We were the gatekeepers, and we very much owned the facts as well. If it said it in the *Wall Street Journal*, *The New York Times*, then that was a fact."[2]

In a sense, she's not wrong. There was a time, not that long ago, when the mainstream media enjoyed a mostly amicable relationship with the public; the public expected the media to present the news in an unbiased, objective manner and in return, gave the media its trust, time, and money.

Still, saying that an industry owns the facts is a bit chilling because the inference is that having possession over the facts means having free rein to manipulate them.

Facts are facts.

Or so we thought. Over a period of several decades, American journalism, once a bastion of freedom, free speech, and democracy, is nearly unrecognizable. Forces and ideologies outside of the newsroom have corrupted and controlled American journalism, mutating it into a screeching, pulsating, sinister creature. The American public has responded with frustration, distrust and downright enmity.

But in saying the quiet part out loud, Tucker's words serve as an indicator of the mindset of journalism moguls across the country. They seem stupefied as to why their metrics and subscriptions are plummeting, why people say they are "fake," why they are forced to shutter or gut newsrooms of key personnel.

To those in the mainstream media, if you want to know what the problem is, look in the mirror. It's you.

The beast is dying, eating itself from within.

How we got to this point took time, though some tried to sound the alarm; unfortunately, no one listened. President Richard M. Nixon warned us about the narcissistic sickness that was overtaking the media and even submitted the reason why it would get worse. In a 1983 interview, he said journalists spend their entire careers putting everyone and everything under the microscope, and as a result, have a very difficult time doing any amount of introspection.[3]

"The problem is that they have a sense of self-righteousness," Nixon said. "They can find everything wrong with somebody else, but they will not look inside and ever admit that they could be wrong themselves."[4]

Almost two decades prior, Nixon's Vice President, Spiro Agnew, delivered a speech in Des Moines, Iowa, and addressed concern about the media's unbridled influence over the American public.[5]

"Nowhere in our system are there fewer checks on such vast power," Agnew said. "So nowhere should there be more conscientious responsibility exercised than by the news media. The question is, 'Are we demanding enough of our television news presentations?'"[6]

There may be fewer "checks" on the American media, but that is necessary for a free press. But the countervailing prospect is that the public is also free to not tune in with their time and their money if they are not pleased with the media's products.

I was a newspaper reporter from 1996-2021. During the latter half of my career, I sensed that the American public was growing increasingly frustrated and distrustful of the media. Later, I became aware of several surveys that backed up my suspicions. Before I left the profession, I sensed the industry was headed sideways to the point that ethically, I wasn't sure I could continue to operate in it.

All of this leads to one question – can the beast be saved?

The answer is, like most things, complicated; but yes, I believe it can. It's going to take time, some deep soul-searching, and probably a fair amount of pain. In this first section, I'll take a look back at history, so that we might arrive at the root causes of the issue, then how those root causes manifested in the decades that followed, and finally, lay out what can be done to remedy the situation.

The other possibility is that the old beast may be allowed to perish, while a new beast will be – and possibly already has been – bred and nurtured by those the public has determined are better equipped to feed it.

---

[1] A conversation with former Wikimedia CEO, Katherine Maher, AtlanticCouncil YouTube channel, https://www.youtube.com/watch?v=y-JRPJnVvOU.

[2] Hoft, Jim. "'We Were the Gatekeepers. We Owned the Facts as Well' - Watch: *Wall Street Journal* Chief Editor Whines About Losing Control of the Narrative at Davos." The Gateway Pundit, January 21, 2024. www.thegatewaypundit.com/2024/01/we-were-gatekeepers-we-owned-facts-as-well/.

3 Richard Nixon Foundation. "President Nixon Warns Against the 'Media Elitist Complex.'" YouTube, January 16, 2024. www.youtube.com/watch?v=TEX6ONLvJg0.

4 Ibid.

5 Eidenmuller, Michael E. "American Rhetoric: Spiro Agnew – Television News Coverage (Nov 13, 1969)." www.americanrhetoric.com/speeches/spiroagnewtvnewscoverage.htm.

6 Ibid.

PART I

DESTRUCTION

Chapter 1 – Decades of Deception

When I first considered the relationship between mainstream media and the public and how it had deteriorated over the past few decades, I realized there wasn't one cause, but several ingredients which, when churned together in a big boiling cauldron, produced a witches' hell-broth of distrust and frustration.

In my journalism school days at the University of Rhode Island, in the early- to mid-1990s, professors wove cautionary tales about defrocked reporters. These poor souls violated journalism ethics by fabricating sources, quotes, and sometimes entire stories. They paid the price, usually in the form of public embarrassment and a pink slip. But their selfish actions carried with them reverberations in the form of shame, not only on their respective newspapers, but to journalism as an institution. These incidents, many of which were front-page news, had a cumulative effect; the public remembers and can only take so much.

It is possible that some of these media transgressors were spellbound by the glamourization of journalism as it was portrayed in movies in the 1970s and '80s. During those decades, a sizeable chunk of highly-acclaimed films featured hardscrabble, charming, or otherwise ethically-driven journalists as their main characters: *The Parallax View*, 1974; *All the President's Men* and *Network*, both in 1976; *Absence of Malice*, 1981, and *Broadcast News*, 1987.

The Unwanted Trailblazer

In J-school, Janet Cooke was *the* cautionary tale; she committed the cardinal sin of journalism – she flat-out concocted a story – and appeared to be among the first in an agonizingly long line of journalistic charlatans. In 1981, after an internal investigation at *The Post*, Cooke admitted that her Pulitzer Prize-winning story, "Jimmy's World" – a feature about an 8-year-old heroin addict – was a total fabrication.[1] In the years that followed, it seemed like a twisted game of whack-a-mole because so many dishonorable reporters were grabbing headlines for all the wrong reasons.

Cooke's story was not only impactful because of its inaugural status, but also because the stakes were so high. The prestigious *Washington Post*, not far removed from the notoriety of Woodward and Bernstein's Watergate investigation, won the prize of all prizes, The Pulitzer, and the story was written about two topics that hit people hard: kids and drugs. And on top of all that, it was written by a black woman, an anomaly in the profession in the early 1980s, and the first to win the vaunted prize.[2]

"And from that moment forward, journalism changed, too," Mike Sager wrote in a 2016 *Columbia Journalism Review* piece. "Cooke became infamous, the first in a line of publicly exposed fabulists including Stephen Glass of The New Republic, Jayson Blair of *The New York Times*, and Jack Kelley of *USA Today*."[3]

Shattered Glass

As Sager mentioned above, another high-profile case involved Stephen Glass, a writer for The New Republic. The revelation and subsequent investigation into Glass' cunning contrivances, followed by layers of deception, were detailed in a 1998 *Vanity Fair* story by Buzz Bissinger.[4]

The story opens with Glass' editor, Charles Lane, desperately hoping to find any shred of truth in the literary labyrinth Glass had constructed. He was met with an elaborate psy-op by Glass, who worked at The New Republic from 1995-1998 and was considered a rising star in the glossy, inside-the-beltway magazine circuit.[5]

"He had appeared wounded, almost outraged," Bissinger wrote. "But Glass was acting; he knew exactly what he had done. Every name, every company, virtually every single solitary detail – except Glass's own byline – had been a product of the young man's imagination."[6]

Glass wrote a novel in 2003, titled *The Fabulist* (tip o' the hat to Sager), in which he explains in the author's note, "While this novel was inspired by certain events in my life, it does not recount the actual events of my life. Instead, it depicts an imaginary world of my own creation. This book is a work of fiction – a fabrication, and this time, an admitted one."[7]

The Blair Affair

In 2003, another major scandal rocked the industry. *New York Times* staff writer Jayson Blair was found to have engineered and plagiarized his way through numerous stories produced for the paper.[8]

The fallout from Blair's transgressions was far-reaching, according to an ethics case study by the Society of Professional Journalists.[9]

"The findings of a 25-member committee headed by Allan Siegal, an assistant managing editor, led to the appointment of a public editor and stricter editorial policies," according to the story on spj.org. "But staffing changes and higher standards could not change what happened: The *Times*' reputation was deeply tarnished. [*Times* Executive Editor Howell] Raines and Managing Editor Gerald Boyd resigned in a cloud of mismanagement. Journalism, in general, suffered perhaps the biggest blow to its credibility in U.S. History."[10]

Chinook Controversy

During the same year as the Blair Affair, NBC News correspondent Brian Williams accompanied troops in Chinook helicopters as they invaded Iraq. The next year, he succeeded the retiring Tom Brokaw as anchor of NBC Nightly News. Williams received the Walter Cronkite Award for Excellence in Journalism in 2009, and not only that, but the GOAT, Walter Cronkite himself, heaped praise on him for his skills and dedication as a "fastidious newsman."[11]

It all started to unravel for Williams in 2015 when he misstated on a Jan. 30 broadcast that the Chinook in which he was a passenger was "forced down after being hit by an RPG."[12] The next month, Williams addressed America and said, "I want to apologize, I said I was in an aircraft that was hit by RPG fire. I was instead in a following aircraft."[13]

The gravity of Williams' words was not lost on NBC executives. They could discern the potentially irreparable harm he had draped on the network's reputation. NBC handed down a six-month suspension without pay and issued some strong words for their now-fallen star.

"By his actions Brian has jeopardized the trust millions of Americans place in NBC News," said Steve Burke, NBC Universal's chief executive. "His actions are inexcusable and this suspension is severe and appropriate."[14]

Williams, upon completing his suspension, was exiled to the network's gulag of sorts, MSNBC, where he was named breaking news anchor. NBC conducted a painstaking investigation into Williams' past decade of work and discovered a pattern of specious information he had spouted about his activities for the network.[15]

"The extensive review found that Williams made a number of inaccurate statements about his own role and experiences covering events in the field," read a network press release.[16]

The Father of Fake News

Growing up in the 1970s and '80s, I remember Walter Cronkite on TV. He was the most trusted man in news, America's grandfather. Everybody loved the guy – rich or poor, Republican or Democrat, man or woman. As Cronkite's successor, Dan Rather was under enormous pressure, but he arrived with a lot of fanfare and a solid reputation, so it appeared he was well-equipped for the job. But Rather's actions on a particular story – driven by hubris, the burden of feeding the beast, or possibly the compulsion to affect a Presidential election – caused him to be bestowed the sobriquet, Father of Fake News.[17]

The year was 2004 and America was gearing up for the Presidential election between Republican incumbent President George W. Bush and Democratic challenger John Kerry. The race's "October Surprise" came a month early, when CBS's *60 Minutes* aired a story hosted by Rather that focused on Bush's military record during the Vietnam War.[18]

During the broadcast, Rather asserted that a group of files known as the Killian documents, produced in 1972, stemmed from files belonging to the late Lt. Col. Jerry B. Killian. It was Killian who commanded Bush during his time in the Texas Air National Guard service and indicated Bush was derelict of his duties on several fronts. All of this, Rather said, was then covered up. The segment was heavily criticized almost immediately after it aired, with Bush allies asserting the story was a hit-piece designed to tip the election in Kerry's favor.[19]

"The report, which lasted fifteen minutes, forever damaged Rather's reputation and ended his network TV career after forty years," wrote Joe Hagan of *Texas Monthly*.[20]

Rather's journalistic maneuvers leading up to the segment turned out to be a lesson in amateur hour; it was more a case of what wasn't done, rather than what was. According to *National Review*, Rather, along with producer Mary Mapes and their team, contended the Killian documents were verified by experts and also the Texas Air National Guard, but such was not the case. Rather and company, as it has been represented, never interviewed anyone who had worked with the now-deceased Killian, and also neglected to compare the 1972 documents with verified memos from the Texas Air National Guard.[21]

About a week after the segment aired, Rather admitted to the big-time botch.

"Now, after extensive additional interviews, I no longer have the confidence in these documents that would allow us to continue vouching for them journalistically," Rather said in a statement dated Sept. 20, 2004. "We made a mistake in judgment, and for that I am sorry. It was an error that was made, however, in good faith and in the spirit of trying to carry on a CBS News tradition of investigative reporting without fear or favoritism."[22]

An independent panel determined that "CBS News failed to follow basic journalistic principles in the preparation and reporting of the piece." Three CBS employees who worked on the segment were asked to resign, while Mapes was fired.[23] Rather's departure was delayed until the next year, when his contract was up and CBS decided not to renew it.[24]

A Hoax on Campus

One of the most infamous media blunders of the 2010s, which had considerable and protracted impact, was the Nov. 19, 2014, story in *Rolling Stone* titled "A Rape on Campus," by Sabrina Rubin Erdely. Erdely's 9,000-word tome wove the story of an alleged 2012 sexual assault of University of Virginia student "Jackie" by a group of fraternity brothers.[25]

The repercussion from the story was a tragic trifecta – to the craft of journalism, to actual rape victims, and to collegiate life across the country, by advocating the existence of an alleged "rape culture."

Erdely's reporting was rife with flaws, including the credibility of the supposed victim, her use of a "cinematic writing style," and the possibility that she did not track down and seek comment from the alleged perpetrators, according to *The Guardian*.[26]

When Erdely's story was published, its popularity hit stratospheric heights and garnered numerous headlines from major media outlets. According to an ABC News story titled "How the Retracted *Rolling Stone* Article 'A Rape on Campus' Came to Print" by Eamon McNiff, Lauren Effron, and Jeff Schneider, "The magazine exposé became the most read non-celebrity story in the 49-year history of *Rolling Stone*."[27] Erdely was profiled by *The Washington Post*, where she firmly defended her story and Jackie's credibility.[28]

ABC's story indicates there were several significant red flags prior to the article's publication, but somehow, *Rolling Stone* pushed forward with it anyway. ABC News was able to procure Erdely's notes and found that Jackie's story evolved during interviews between the two.[29]

Not long after its publication, as the tale began to unravel, *Rolling Stone* requested that Steve Coll, then-Dean of the Columbia School of Journalism, conduct an audit of Erdley's reporting and the subsequent editing and fact-checking that occurred at the magazine.[30]

"This report was painful reading, to me personally and to all of us at *Rolling Stone*. It is also, in its own way, a fascinating document – a piece of journalism, as Coll describes it, about a failure of journalism. With its publication, we are officially retracting 'A Rape on Campus.' We are also committing ourselves to a series of recommendations about journalistic practices that are spelled out in the report. We would like to apologize to our readers and to all of those who were damaged by our story and the ensuing fallout," wrote Will Dana, then-managing editor of *Rolling Stone*.[31]

Tip of the Iceberg

In 2007, Randall Hoven of *The American Thinker* compiled what he described as a "scorecard" of journalistic bungles, botches, and blunders. Hoven said the impetus for his list was the Scott Thomas Beauchamp controversy. Beauchamp, a former military officer, penned several essays for The New Republic that detailed alleged despicable actions by soldiers in Iraq. The U.S. Army launched an investigation and concluded the essays were fabricated[32] and The New Republic also initiated an internal investigation.[33]

"Since this controversy began, The New Republic's sole objective has been to uncover the truth," according to New Republic Staff.[34] The outlet concluded in December 2007, that "in light of the evidence available to us, after months of intensive re-reporting, we cannot be confident that the events in his pieces occurred in exactly the manner that he described them. Without that essential confidence, we cannot stand by these stories."[35]

In Hoven's column, he compiled 62 journalists, columnists, and their indiscretions, concluding with, "If this is the visible part of the iceberg, just how big is the iceberg?"[36]

[1] Meyer, Gene. "Recalling 'Jimmy's World' at *The Washington Post*." March 25, 2021. eugenelmeyer.com/2021/03/25/recalling-jimmys-world-at-the-washington-post/.

[2] Fulker, Rick. "Marking History: The Pulitzer Prize." Deutsche Welle, May 9, 2022. www.dw.com/en/marking-history-the-pulitzer-prize/a-43400313#:~:text=In%201981%2C%20Janet%20Cooke%20was%20the%20first%20African-American,a%20national%20outpouring%20of%20sympathy%20for%20the%20boy.

[3] Sager, Mike. "The Fabulist Who Changed Journalism." *Columbia Journalism Review*. www.cjr.org/the_feature/the_fabulist_who_changed_journalism.php.

[4] Bissinger, Buzz. "Shattered Glass." *Vanity Fair*, September 5, 2007. www.vanityfair.com/magazine/1998/09/bissinger199809.

[5] Ibid.

[6] Ibid.

[7] Kirkpatrick, David D. "A History of Lying Recounted as Fiction." *The New York Times*, May 7, 2003. www.nytimes.com/2003/05/07/books/a-history-of-lying-recounted-as-fiction.html.

[8] Uribarri, Adrian. "Ethics Case Studies: The Times and Jason Blair." SPJ Ethics Committee, Society of Professional Journalists. www.spj.org/ecs13.asp.

[9] Ibid.

[10] Ibid.

[11] Siegel, Ed. "A Matter of Trust: Brian Williams' Conflate-Gate and Jon Stewart's Departure." WBUR News, February 11, 2015. www.wbur.org/news/2015/02/11/stewart-williams.

[12] Sen, Sumanti. "A Look Back at the Brian Williams 'Fake War Story' Controversy." Meaww.com, November 10, 2021. meaww.com/a-look-back-at-the-brian-williams-fake-war-story-controversy.

[13] McCarthy, Tom, and agencies. "NBC's Brian Williams Forced to Retract Story About Coming Under Fire in Iraq." *The Guardian*, February 5, 2015. www.theguardian.com/world/2015/feb/04/brian-williams-forced-retract-feel-good-iraq-war-story-10-years-later.

[14] "NBC News Anchor Brian Williams Suspended 6 Months Without Pay." CBS News, February 11, 2015. www.cbsnews.com/news/nbc-news-anchor-brian-williams-suspended-6-months-without-pay/.

15 Stelloh, Tim. "Longtime Anchor Brian Williams Leaving NBC after 28 Years." NBCNews.com, November 9, 2021. www.nbcnews.com/news/us-news/longtime-anchor-brian-williams-leaving-nbc-28-years-rcna5042.

16 Pallotta, Frank. "NBC's Brian Williams Investigation: What We Know." CNNMoney, June 18, 2015. http://money.cnn.com/2015/06/18/media/brian-williams-nbc-investigation/index.html.

17 Bedard, Paul. "Dan Rather Calls for End of Balanced News." *Washington Examiner*, March 5, 2024. https://gazette.com/news/wex/dan-rather-calls-for-end-of-balanced-news/article_50232807-606b-5781-b5c9-c44c96174d6a.html.

18 Hagan, Joe. "Truth or Consequences." *Texas Monthly*, May 2012. www.texasmonthly.com/news-politics/truth-or-consequences/.

19 Ibid.

20 Ibid.

21 Geraghty, Jim. "Dan Rather Still Insists His Anti-Bush Memo Story from 2004 Was True." *National Review*, October 13, 2015. www.nationalreview.com/corner/dan-rather-still-insists-his-anti-bush-memo-story-2004-was-true-jim-geraghty/.

22 Murphy, Jarrett. "Dan Rather Statement on Memos." CBS News, September 20, 2004. www.cbsnews.com/news/dan-rather-statement-on-memos/.

23 Murphy, Jarrett. "CBS Ousts 4 for Bush Guard Story." CBS News, January 10, 2005. www.cbsnews.com/news/cbs-ousts-4-for-bush-guard-story-10-01-2005/.

24 CBS News. "Dan Rather Signs Off: Veteran Newsman Exits CBS after 44 Years with Tiffany Network." CBS News, June 20, 2006. web.archive.org/web/20060622105927/https://www.cbsnews.com/stories/2006/06/19/national/main1727285.shtml.

25 Erdely, Sabrina Rubin. "A Rape on Campus: A Brutal Assault and Struggle for Justice at UVA." *Rolling Stone*, November 19, 2014. http://web.archive.org/web/20141119200349/http://www.rollingstone.com/culture/features/a-rape-on-campus-20141119.

26 Graves, Lucia. "Five Years on, the Lessons from the *Rolling Stone* Rape Story." *The Guardian*, December 29, 2019. www.theguardian.com/society/2019/dec/29/rolling-stone-rape-story-uva-five-years.

27 McNiff, Eamon, et al. "How the Retracted *Rolling Stone* Article 'A Rape on Campus' Came to Print." ABC News. http://abcnews.go.com/2020/deepdive/how-retracted-rolling-stone-article-rape-on-campus-came-print-42701166.

[28] Farhi, Paul. "Sabrina Rubin Erdely, Woman Behind *Rolling Stone*'s Explosive ..." *Washington Post*, November 28, 2014. https://www.washingtonpost.com/lifestyle/style/sabrina-rubin-erdely-woman-behind-rolling-stones-explosive-u-va-alleged-rape-story/2014/11/28/89f322c2-7731-11e4-bd1b-03009bd3e984_story.html.

[29] McNiff, Eamon, et al. "How the Retracted *Rolling Stone* Article 'A Rape on Campus' Came to Print." ABC News. http://abcnews.go.com/2020/deepdive/how-retracted-rolling-stone-article-rape-on-campus-came-print-42701166.

[30] Coronel, Sheila, et al. "*Rolling Stone*'s Investigation: 'A Failure That Was Avoidable.'" *Columbia Journalism Review*, April 5, 2015. https://www.cjr.org/investigation/rolling_stone_investigation.php.

[31] Hartmann, Margaret. "*Rolling Stone* Retracts UVA Rape Story Following Report on 'Journalistic Failure.'" *New York Magazine*, Intelligencer, April 5, 2015. http://nymag.com/intelligencer/2015/04/rolling-stone-retracts-uva-rape-story.html.

[32] Hoven, Randall. "It's Not Just Scott Beauchamp." americanthinker.com, August 16, 2007. https://www.americanthinker.com/articles/2007/08/its_not_just_scott_beauchamp.html.

[33] "A Scott Beauchamp Update." The New Republic, October 26, 2007. http://newrepublic.com/article/33094/scott-beauchamp-update.

[34] Ibid.

[35] Foer, Franklin. "Fog of War." The New Republic, December 10, 2007. https://newrepublic.com/article/65683/fog-war.

[36] Hoven, Randall. "It's Not Just Scott Beauchamp." americanthinker.com, August 16, 2007. https://www.americanthinker.com/articles/2007/08/its_not_just_scott_beauchamp.html.

Chapter 2 – 24 Hours Is Not Enough

If there were any more hours that could be squeezed into the 24-hour news cycle, pioneering media titans would have found a way. But by establishing such a machine, were they merely reacting to people's changing appetites for news consumption, or did they trigger it? We may never know, but here we are.

The 24-hour news cycle as we know it today was an accident, some say. Enter maverick mogul Ted Turner, who began scarfing up television stations in the late 1960s, one of which was Atlanta's WTCG.[1]

As the story goes, Turner was not a big hard news fan, but the Federal Communications Commission declared it mandatory for all television stations to "do a certain amount of public service broadcasting news," according to Lisa Napoli, author of *Up All Night: Ted Turner, CNN, and the Birth of 24-Hour News*. Begrudgingly, Turner produced a late-night tongue-in-cheek newscast because he didn't think anyone would be watching at that time.[2]

In 1980, he launched the Cable News Network. CNN's impact is indisputable – it spawned many competitors, including MSNBC, FOX News, HLN (formerly CNN Headline News), FOX Business, and The Weather Channel, to name a few.

CNN is viewed as a trailblazing enterprise in many respects, but will also be regarded in infamy for creating a media tail-wagging-the-dog scenario. In 1992, U.S. President George Walker Bush came under scrutiny when he green-lit the deployment of soldiers to Somalia after he saw coverage on

CNN of malnourished refugees caught in a conflict between two rival warlords. And so "The CNN Effect" was born.³

"Were American interests really at stake? Was CNN deciding where the military goes next?" Margaret Belknap wrote.⁴

Bush's decision was sandwiched between two other major events that Redstate at Townhall Editor-at-Large Kira Ayn Davis said cemented the 24/7 news cycle as a cultural cornerstone – the U.S. invasion of Iraq in 1991 and the O.J. Simpson murder trial in 1994-95.⁵

"Those were two sensational events that drew people to their TVs," Davis said on the Cruel Philosophr TikTok account. "It was drama, it was war, it was popular football player, it was murder, it was all of these things and the television industry began to respond, so that's how we got what we now know as the 24-hour cable network conglomerate."⁶

It is possible that once the real-life, real-time soap opera that was the O.J. Simpson trial concluded, the public's thirst reached a new high, and so the relationship between viewers and news providers became a symbiotic one. The genie was out of the bottle, never to be stuffed back in again. Now imagine injecting the concept of the 24-hour news cycle with a fresh syringe of steroids, and bam, you've got the internet. With cable, viewers were spoon-fed chunks of news, but online, it was administered in rapid-fire morsels, as if from a virtual Gatling gun.

The O.J. Simpson trial also served to mark a second era of Yellow Journalism in the U.S., at times referred to as "Tabloid Journalism" or "Sensationalism." The original era of Yellow Journalism refers to a period in the 1890s where the two New York newspaper titans, William Randolph Hearst and Joseph Pulitzer, pitched a no-holds-barred battle against each other for media domination in America.

In another opinion, David Kamp, in a *Vanity Fair* story written at the end of the 1990s, cites the July 26, 1991, arrest of Pee-wee Herman actor Paul Reubens – caught masturbating at the South Trail Cinema in Sarasota, Florida – as the beginning of the decade of sensationalism.[7]

"But something about the Pee-wee situation was new: the immediate Topic A-ness of his arrest, the countrywide mirth at his humiliation, the play the story got in proportion to its significance, the phony undercurrent of parental concern, the veritable carnival the whole thing mushroomed into," Kamp wrote.[8]

Still others say sensationalism began with the first live police pursuit in 1992, shot by helicopter pilot then-Bob (now Zoey) Tur and wife Marika, who operated a video camera. The chase rivaled anything Hollywood was cranking out at the time – a devil-may-care murderer leading Los Angeles's finest on a high-speed hunt across highways, with the city's citizens in danger of becoming collateral damage. The result was not only a ratings bonanza, but the advent of an innovative journalism trend – aerial police chase footage – that persisted for decades to come, according to the Los Angeles Almanac.[9]

The *Los Angeles Times* put the story across the top of its front page, above the fold and dubbed it "a marriage of technology and tragedy," according to Buzzfeed.[10]

If the televised police chase of 1992 is to be considered the inaugural moment that birthed the public's ravenous nature for sensational real-time events, the 1994 O.J. Simpson slow-speed police chase in the infamous white Ford Bronco was the incident that solidified it for decades to come.

"On TV, the chase was simply inescapable," according to CNN. "Some 95 million people watched the chase that night, and they watched it in a way that we don't watch events now. People stood in large groups in front of televisions in their homes, bars, restaurants and other public places and just gawked at the spectacle."[11]

Some individuals, like Hollywood director John Carpenter, saw the dawn of sensationalism on the horizon. Carpenter's 1988 film *They Live* is a harbinger of what the horror director viewed as the pervading zeitgeist of the decade, eating away at the fabric of society and the impending results if it wasn't mitigated.

His protagonist, played by professional wrestler "Rowdy" Roddy Piper, unwittingly discovers that aliens have infiltrated the echelons of power in America and are controlling the masses with subliminal messages commanding them to "obey" and "sleep." The nefarious invaders transmit their messages through television, as they discover that media is an effective method to manipulate the masses. The result of their fiendish plot is unbridled greed among earthlings, the elevation of celebrity to deity-like status, and an ever-widening chasm between the rich and the poor.

It's also a heck of an action movie, which birthed the enduring line, "I have come here to chew bubblegum and kick ass… and I'm all out of bubblegum."[12]

Now imagine the 24-hour news cycle, consumers' exacerbated thirst for news, the rise of sensationalism, and then add in an entirely new vehicle to communicate – the internet.

From my perspective as a reporter in the late 1990s, it seemed that newspapers were dragged kicking-and-screaming into the digital age. Most media owners and editors initially looked at the internet as a fad, the medium *du jour* with which people would soon be bored, or possibly another tool in the toolbox, but certainly not a revolutionary one.

"The truth is no online database will replace your daily newspaper, no CD-ROM can take the place of a competent teacher and no computer network will change the way government works," astronomer Clifford Stoll wrote in 1995.[13]

In short, newspapers were slow to establish websites and when they finally did get online, few constructed "pay walls" – virtual restrictions to content only accessed by paid subscription.

"Very few newspapers could afford or had the expertise to create online outlets, nor was there much desire to," wrote Amit Rathore in a Mashable story. "The investments required to build out websites were steep, with Time Warner's celebrated Pathfinder site reputedly costing $120 million to build. The audience was, at that time, very limited."[14]

In 1980, Bob Johnson, then-vice president of the *Columbus Dispatch*, took a measured approach to the fledgling internet. "We do think that it provides us with an excellent means to supplement the daily newspaper, by providing readers with updated information, after they receive their paper, throughout the day, so that any time during the day that a reader wants the latest story, the latest bit of information on a particular item, all they have to do is dial into the CompuServe service," Johnson said.[15]

The *Columbus Dispatch* may have been the first newspaper to offer an e-edition with CompuServe, but that was while still cranking out a daily physical newspaper. In the 2000s, we saw daily papers decrease the number of publication days per week. Whoever heard of a daily newspaper not publishing daily? Then you had *The Christian Science Monitor*, which transitioned to a strictly online version in 2009.[16]

Looking back, it's almost a perfect storm that developed organically – the emergence of the 24-hour news cycle, the evolution of the internet, combined with major salacious events

— created a shrinking short-attention span among viewers and readers. The media had the keys to the kingdom, but as we have seen and will see, unbridled power begat an enveloping malfeasance.

---

[1] Smith, Ernie. "Ted Turner Was the Steve Jobs of Television, and That's Not Hyperbole." Tedium, May 7, 2015. http://tedium.co/2015/05/07/ted-turner-tbs-superstation-history/.

[2] Hobson, Jeremy. "How Ted Turner's Vision for CNN Sparked the 24-Hour News Cycle." WBUR, Here & Now, May 12, 2020. www.wbur.org/hereandnow/2020/05/12/cnn-ted-turner-lisa-napoli.

[3] Benabid, Kaouthar. "What Is the CNN Effect and Why Is It Relevant Today?" Al Jazeera Media Institute, February 22, 2021. https://institute.aljazeera.net/en/ajr/article/1365.

[4] Belknap, Margaret H. "The CNN Effect: Strategic Enabler or Operational Risk?" USAWC Press, March 30, 2001. https://www.semanticscholar.org/paper/The-CNN-Effect%3A-Strategic-Enabler-or-Operational-Belknap/92b15823b7bf6521bb62271271b386123e8707d5

[5] CruelPhilosophr. "Did Traditional Media Cause Today's Political Turmoil?" YouTube, June 27, 2023. https://www.youtube.com/watch?v=vc98o-y-gtk.

[6] Ibid.

[7] Kamp, David. "The Tabloid Decade." *Vanity Fair*, February 7, 1999. https://www.vanityfair.com/culture/1999/02/david-kamp-tabloid-decade.

[8] Ibid.

[9] "First Televised Police Pursuit Los Angeles County." Los Angeles Almanac. https://www.laalmanac.com/crime/cr724.php.

[10] Testa, Jessica. "Why Did Jordon Romero Kill Himself on Live Television?" BuzzFeed, May 9, 2013. https://www.buzzfeed.com/jtes/why-did-jodon-romero-kill-himself-on-live-television.

[11] Criss, Doug. "25 Years Ago Today, America Stopped to Watch the Cops Chase O.J. in a White Ford Bronco." CNN, June 17, 2019. https://www.cnn.com/2019/06/17/us/oj-simpson-car-chase-anniversary-trnd/index.html.

[12] Movieclips. "They Live (1988): Here to Chew Bubble Gum and Kick Ass Scene (4/10)." YouTube, August 26, 2019. https://www.youtube.com/watch?v=Du5YK5FnyF4&t=12s.

[13] Stoll, Clifford. "Why the Web Won't Be Nirvana." *Newsweek*, February 26, 1995. https://www.newsweek.com/clifford-stoll-why-web-wont-be-nirvana-185306.

[14] Rathore, Amit. "Dialing Up the Past: How Did the Early Internet Affect the Media?" Mashable, January 30, 2017. https://mashable.com/article/how-early-internet-affected-media.

[15] Smith, Ernie. "Early Efforts to Bring the News Online Changed the Shape of Media Forever." *Vice*, November 9, 2016. https://www.vice.com/en/article/53dqjn/early-efforts-to-bring-the-news-online-changed-the-shape-of-media-forever.

[16] Clifford, Stephanie. "Christian Science Paper to End Daily Print Edition." *The New York Times*, October 28, 2008. https://www.nytimes.com/2008/10/29/business/media/29paper.html.

Chapter 3 – The Disregard of Objectivity

"If the journalism gods wanted you to have opinions, they would have given them to you when you graduated from J-school." —Ted Czech

For the past couple decades, certain influential factions in journalism have embraced and propagated the renunciation of one of the main tenets of the profession – objectivity. And as someone who enjoyed (well, mostly enjoyed) a 25-year-career in the field, I think I can safely say that disregard of objectivity is an abject failure. Let's take a look at some examples of how this ideology has taken hold.

Kathleen McElroy, who was hired as a professor at the University of Texas at Austin campus to revive its journalism program in June 2023, uncorked this number that some say led to the paring-down of the university's offer to her, which originally included tenure.[1]

"We can't just give people a set of facts anymore," McElroy said in an AP story. "I think we know that and we have to tell our students that. This is not about getting two sides of a story or three sides of a story, if one side is illegitimate. I think now you cannot cover education, you cannot cover criminal justice, you can't cover all of these institutions without realizing how all these institutions were built."[2]

Then we have Anita Varma, one of McElroy's co-workers, who penned a piece for the Nieman Lab in 2021 titled "Solidarity Eclipses Objectivity as Journalism's Dominant Ideal."[3] In it, Varma advocates journalists eschewing objectivity for what she calls solidarity. A link in her essay leads to a definition on mediaengagement.org, which she is credited as the researcher, that reads, "Solidarity is 'a commitment to social justice that translates into action.'"[4]

In Varma's essay, she submits that solidarity is a far more noble and effective goal than objectivity for journalists, and uses the example of a reporter looking out the window and seeing rain, but not being able to determine why it is raining, the origins of the rain, or its implications.[5]

"Striving for objectivity, then, leads journalism to a dead end," Varma writes. "On the other hand, an ideal and method of solidarity for social justice is much more aligned with what the best journalists have always tried to do: inform the public of issues that matter, hold institutional power accountable, and challenge society to be better by urging us to care about more than ourselves."[6]

Varma's solidarity detours the profession of journalism in a direction it was never intended or designed to go. If you want to talk true solidarity, look at the Polish movement of the same name in the 1980s. Led by Lech Wałęsa – who won the Nobel Peace Prize for his leadership and vision – "Solidarność" was a 10-million person strong, non-violent movement that advocated for workers' rights and contributed to the end of communism in the country.[7] This revolutionary movement advanced the type of social justice of which Varma speaks, but it is nonsensical to take the principles of a social movement and apply them to a vehicle such as journalism, the purpose of which is to chronicle history as it happens, not champion one cause over another.

But that is apparently what journalism programs at American colleges, along with support from some major figures in journalism, have attempted to do.

After CNN hosted the Trump Town Hall on May 10, 2023, the network's Christiane Amanpour spoke to a group of Columbia Journalism School graduates later the same month.

"Be truthful, but not neutral," Amanpour advised the graduates. "Bothsidesism is not always objectivity. It does not get you to the truth. Drawing false moral or factual equivalence is neither objective or truthful."[8]

Months later, in an interview with CNN, Amanpour stated she developed her "be truthful, not neutral" line after interviewing President Bill Clinton on the war in Bosnia.[9]

"Everybody was trying to say both sides are equally guilty. And they weren't. They are not, like they are not in Russia and Ukraine right now. And also, in climate change. So, on every issue, be truthful, not neutral."[10]

But here's the rub – who elected journalists like Amanpour to be the ultimate arbiters of right and wrong? In her example, were journalists the adjudicators of which side assumed more guilt than the other? Russia-Ukraine, just like Israel-Palestine, is complicated. Knowing who is in the right and the wrong, well, that depends on to whom you pose the question. There are people all over the world who believe Russia has every right to invade Ukraine – saying that countries have invaded other countries for thousands of years – or, on another level, remain ambivalent over the matter.[11] Same with climate change. There are journalists who write that 97 percent of climate experts believe humans are principally responsible for global warming, while other research shows that number to be considerably lower, and many experts propose that humans have played a negligible role in climate change.[12] Most journalists are not climate experts, so they should approach the issue with curiosity and balance, not fanaticism and injudiciousness. There are those who are staunch advocates for solar and wind power measures, while others submit the practices can cause considerable harm to wildlife and their habitats and require plastic, metal, lye, and hydrofluoric acid to construct.[13]

In a double-whammy post on X on March 4, 2024, Dan Rather, letting his politics get the better of him, deployed not only "both-sides-ism," but also the over-used propaganda term "democracy."[14]

"Enough with Both-sides-ism," Rather wrote, "when one side lies intentionally and repeatedly, they are no longer entitled to the benefit of the doubt. They should be held to account, right away. Do not simply repeat the narratives they spew ... Ask Lawmakers Hard Questions. Ask about the fundamental principles of democracy. Push them to go on the record that Biden won the 2020 election."[15]

Looking at these examples, it seems the crux of the issue is that McElroy, Varma, Amanpour, Rather, and others desire journalism to be something that it cannot be. Journalism is not political advocacy or social activism.

Proponents of this "advocacy" or "solidarity" journalism are attempting to artificially inseminate activism – which is, at its core, partisanship – into true journalism; and overwhelmingly, as we will see in the next section, the host body has rejected the parasite.

McElroy, along with Amanpour and Rather's favorite non-word, "both-sides-ism," floats the idea that presenting opposing sides of a story, however many there may be, is disingenuous, "if one side is illegitimate." But who is to say if one side is "illegitimate?" Certainly not the journalist. What authority does the journalist possess to be a gatekeeper for things legitimate and illegitimate with regard to their readership? What an insulting prospect, to suggest that readers do not possess the intelligence to use critical thinking.

Say, for example, that Trump, or any other politician, says the sky is green, as Rather puts it; well then, as part of the process of journalism, the reporter has to "repeat the narrative" in order to plainly state to the audience what he is saying. Then, the reporter challenges, "But Mr. Trump, it's a widely-held belief that the sky is blue," and you record Trump's retort and then seek the opinions of others, both for and against what color the sky is, and you present all of that to the audience.

Journalism is no different than any other profession in that emotion and personal ideologies must be set aside to achieve success. A teacher may not agree with a segment of the curriculum, but she teaches it anyway, because it is required of her. A cop may disagree with issuing you a ticket if you exceed the speed limit, but he dispenses it anyway because his job dictates he must. A doctor may not want to perform surgery on the scumbag who just opened fire on a crowd of innocent bystanders, but she swore an oath to do no harm.

Displaying favoritism to one side or another, as Amanpour suggests, effectively sows discontent and distrust between the journalist and their readership. If you are not neutral, as she suggests, you are by definition partisan. On the contrary, the journalist should be the conduit between an issue, an incident, a controversy, and their readership. There is room for activism in journalism, but it comes in the form of columns and editorials.

And so, presenting both or all sides of an argument is the closest damn thing journalists can get to pure objectivity. It gives the power to the people, where it was and always should be. As a journalist, lay out everything you can for the reader and walk away. Leave them a veritable charcuterie board of information from which they can freely eat. Then your audience does its own work, if it wants, and makes its own conclusions. If a journalist is not neutral, then he is, by default, biased, prejudiced, or one-sided. And if he is biased, prejudiced, or one-sided, that is not being truthful. And that is not journalism.

Objectivity is not a dirty word.

---

[1] Sylvester, Sherry. "The Smoking Gun in Texas A&M Journalism Flap." Texas Public Policy Foundation, July 27, 2023. https://www.texaspolicy.com/the-smoking-gun-in-texas-am-journalism-flap/.

[2] Vertuno, Jim. "Texas A&M University President Resigns after Black Journalist's Hiring at Campus Unravels." AP News, July 21, 2023. https://apnews.com/article/texas-am-diversity-inclusion-487edd40ee9a57faa0cfe94e8e4684e6.

[3] Varma, Anita. "Solidarity Eclipses Objectivity as Journalism's Dominant Ideal." NiemanLab, Predictions for Journalism 2022. https://www.niemanlab.org/2021/12/solidarity-eclipses-objectivity-as-journalisms-dominant-ideal/.

[4] Varma, Anita. "Solidarity Reporting Guide." Center for Media Engagement, November 10, 2021. https://mediaengagement.org/research/solidarity-reporting-guide/.

[5] Varma, Anita. "Solidarity Eclipses Objectivity as Journalism's Dominant Ideal." NiemanLab, Predictions for Journalism 2022. https://www.niemanlab.org/2021/12/solidarity-eclipses-objectivity-as-journalisms-dominant-ideal/.

[6] Ibid.

[7] Bartkowski, Maciej. "Poland's Solidarity Movement (1980-1989)." ICNC, December 2009. https://www.nonviolent-conflict.org/polands-solidarity-movement-1980-1989/.

[8] 68.   Bahney, Jennifer Bowers. "Christiane Amanpour Recalls Moment She Came Up with 'Be Truthful, Not Neutral' Mantra She Used to Criticize New CNN Regime." Mediaite, September 12, 2023. https://www.mediaite.com/media/christiane-amanpour-recalls-moment-she-came-up-with-be-truthful-not-neutral-mantra-she-used-to-criticize-new-cnn-regime/.

[9] Ibid.

[10] Ibid.

[11] Davis, Elliott. "Explainer: Why Did Russia Invade Ukraine?" *US News & World Report*, February 23, 2024. https://www.usnews.com/news/best-countries/articles/explainer-why-did-russia-invade-ukraine.

[12] McKitrick, Ross. "Putting the 'con' in Consensus; Not Only Is There No 97 Percent Consensus Among Climate Scientists, Many Misunderstand Core Issues: Op-Ed." Fraser Institute, May 2015. https://www.fraserinstitute.org/article/putting-the-con-in-consensus-not-only-is-there-no-97-per-cent-consensus-among-climate-scientists-many-misunderstand-core-issues.

[13] Fitzner, Zach. "The Environmental Impacts of Solar and Wind Energy." Earth.com, December 5, 2018. https://www.earth.com/news/environmental-impacts-solar-wind-energy/.

[14] Rather, Dan. "If I May, There's Something I Need to Get off My Chest..." Twitter, March 4, 2024. https://twitter.com/DanRather/status/1764821704457495015?ref_src=twsrc%5Etfw%7Ctwcamp%5Etweetembed%7Ctwterm%5E1764821704457495015%7Ctwgr%5E2619029e4140ed4faf45c0b318867980bbc2acdf%7Ctwcon%5Es1_&ref_url=https%3A%2F%2Fwww.washingtonexaminer.com%2Fnews%2F2902755%2Fdan-rather-calls-end-balanced-news%2F.

[15] Ibid.

Chapter 4 – The Rise of Reporter-activists

As a result of generations of young journalism graduates, indoctrinated with the toxins of solidarity or advocacy journalism being discharged into the industry, the consequence has been sort of a mutation – by all appearances a journalist, but lurking underneath, a bitter, malevolent activist.

WaPo Picks the Wrong Target

Here's something I was never taught in J-school – allegedly acting as a political/social saboteur with the intent of damaging not only a person's reputation, but also their profession. But whomever is teaching this sort of subterfuge left out a key detail: Choose your targets carefully or be prepared for a counterstrike. Enter Dave Portnoy, the outspoken leader of Barstool Sports, a website fueled by bawdy humor, testosterone, and flipping the bird at political correctness. In September 2023, Portnoy planned an event he called "Pizzafest" in New York City. However, prior to its launch, *Washington Post* reporter Emily Heil allegedly emailed the event's sponsors. The emails, it seems, were designed to shame the sponsors, possibly into pulling out of the event, implying that perceived public pressure was mounting against them.

"We are planning to write about the festival and how some of the sponsors and participants have drawn criticism by seeming to associate themselves with Dave Portnoy, who has a history of misogynistic comments and other problematic behavior," Heil wrote. "I wanted to make sure that [fill in the blank – company name] had a chance to respond to this, since the company is the most prominent of the 'partners' for his festival."[1]

Wow. If that email was a goblet, the sheer hostility and haughtiness contained within would be bubbling over the brim.

Once Portnoy caught wind of the *Post*'s "hit piece" as he called it – but before they contacted him – he flipped the script and called Heil. Portnoy, while recording the conversation, asked her repeatedly why she felt compelled to focus on his purported "misogynistic comments and other problematic behavior," rather than asking sponsors to comment on, say, the positive things he has done for the food service industry. That's when Heil uncorked this gem: "It's sort of a reporting tactic when you want someone to respond, you kind of have to indicate there might be something negative, and then you get them to engage."[2]

Now that sounds like a CIA-level interrogation right there. It's slick, because there's an underlying implication of humiliation and coercion without coming right out and saying, "If you don't agree to an interview – and during that interview bend the knee and actually pull your sponsorship – your reputation and livelihood will be ruined." If you as a reporter can't get someone to agree to an interview by simply asking them, you don't deserve to call yourself a reporter. If someone refuses to be interviewed, it is their right. Then you state that in your story and readers can interpret for themselves whether that means anything.

Portnoy was disgusted as well, saying to Heil, "That is a sad state of journalism if that's a tactic. So you're leading with something that you haven't done enough research to know if it's valid."[3] Heil seemed unmoved by Portnoy's protestations, continuing to set up a time when she could interview him for the story. The interview never happened, but the hit piece was published and Portnoy countered with a news release, in which he stated, "Today marks the official death of honest and fair journalism in America."4

Proud of Provy

There's an old *Seinfeld* episode where Kramer attends an AIDS walk, but the event's organizers are adamant that he wear a ribbon. Kramer is there to support the cause, but his counter-culture character won't allow him to do something just because everyone else is.

"You know what you are? You're a ribbon-bully," he says to one woman.5

Later in the episode, Kramer is tracked down by the mob and when he remains steadfast in his ribbon-resistance, they set upon him. So, I imagine Kramer would've been proud of his real-life counterpart, hockey player Ivan Provorov, who was accosted online for his own brand of defiance.

On Jan. 17, 2023, Provorov, a Philadelphia Flyers defenseman and practicing Russian Orthodox Christian, refused to wear an LGBT-themed jersey as his team was warming up on the ice. Provorov didn't offer his reasons, he just quietly sat out the session. But journalist-activists seized on it, including Flyers Nation, which bills itself as "an officially credentialed media outlet of the Philadelphia Flyers." An editorial on the site – and from a search on the site, the only article written about the incident – called Provorov's stance "disgraceful."6

"I respect everybody and I respect everybody's choices," Provorov said following the game, according to Fox29 in Philadelphia. "My choice is to stay true to myself and my religion."7

The principle of inclusivity appears not to be absolute, as apparently it does not include one's decision *not* to participate in something, or possibly there is a hidden hierarchy, where sexual orientation is valued above religion.

Steph Driver, NHL Editorial Manager for @SBNation, which is owned by Vox Media, tweeted from her account, @StephaliciousD:

> "Ivan Provorov was allowed to play in a game for the Philadelphia Flyers – the organization that was the first to say that you will be removed from the arena if you utter a homophobic slur – after refusing to wear a Pride logo for warm ups. What an absolute disgrace."[8]

Aside from fans criticizing Driver for her authoritarian viewpoint,[9] I wonder if she thought it was acceptable for Colin Kaepernick to do his whole kneeling stunt in the NFL. The fact that she was even expressing an opinion under the guise of journalism was not lost on some.

Then another NHL journalist, Pierre LeBrun, chimed in on Twitter with "But Provorov obviously does not respect 'everyone.' If he did respect everyone, he would have taken part in warm-up and worn the Pride Night jersey. Don't hide behind religion."[10]

Like Driver, LeBrun experienced some serious push-back on Twitter, with user @Joe_in_NJ tweeting, "To all you young sports fans – go out to youtube and rumble and find sportswriters who love sports. So many of these Lebrun type characters want to use sports as a vehicle to push their own (wacky) politics. Don't even bother with them."[11]

---

[1] Heim, Mark. "Here's Barstool CEO Dave Portnoy calling out *Washington Post* reporter on 'hit piece'." al.com, Sept. 21, 2023.
https://www.al.com/life/2023/09/heres-barstool-ceo-dave-portnoy-calling-out-washington-post-reporter-on-hit-piece.html#:~:text=%E2%80%9CWe%20are%20planning%20to%20write,%2C%E2%80%9D%20Portnoy%20reads%20to%20her.

[2] Ibid.

[3] Ibid.

4 Smokes, Tommy. "For Immediate Release from Team Portnoy: Journalism Is Dead." BarstoolSports, Sept. 22, 2023. https://www.barstoolsports.com/blog/3485774/for-immediate-release-from-team-portnoy-journalism-is-dead.

5 TBS. "Seinfeld: Ribbon (CLIP)." YouTube, July 1, 2014. https://www.youtube.com/watch?v=y4bmGekgE14.

6 Modugno, Jake. "Ivan Provorov's Refusal to Wear a Pride Jersey Is Disgraceful." Flyers Nation, January 17, 2023. https://www.flyersnation.com/ivan-provorovs-refusal-to-wear-a-pride-jersey-is-disgraceful/.

7 Gelston, Dan. "'My Choice Is to Stay True to Myself': Flyers' Provorov Cites Religion for Boycott on Pride Night." FOX 29 News Philadelphia, January 18, 2023. https://www.fox29.com/sports/true-to-myself-flyers-ivan-provorov-cites-religion-boycott-pride-night.

8 Driver, Steph. "Ivan Provorov Was Allowed to Play in a Game for the Philadelphia Flyers – the Organization That Was the First to Say That You Will Be Removed from the Arena If You Utter a Homophobic Slur – After Refusing to Wear a Pride Logo for Warm Ups. What an Absolute Disgrace." Twitter, January 17, 2023. https://twitter.com/StephaliciousD/status/1615541057759870977.

9 Ibid.

10 LeBrun, Pierre. "But Provorov Obviously Does Not Respect 'Everyone'. If He Did Respect Everyone, He Would Have Taken Part in Warm-up and Worn the Pride Night Jersey. Don't Hide behind Religion. Https://T.Co/Qk6dtganmp." Twitter, January 17, 2023. https://twitter.com/PierreVLeBrun/status/1615555931453939712?ref_src=twsrc%255Etfw%257Ctwcamp%255Etweetembed%257Ctwterm%255E1615555931453939712%257Ctwgr%255Eeab3abbaef621feaf82c4ee60defb2cc45ed9faf%257Ctwcon%255Es1_&ref_url=https%253A%252F%252Fwww.foxnews.com%252Fsports%252Fflyers-ivan-provorov-labeled-homophobic-faces-backlash-boycotting-teams-pride-fetivities.

11 Joe, @Joe_in_NJ. "To All You Young Sports Fans – Go out to YouTube and Rumble and Find Sportswriters Who Love Sports. So Many of These Lebrun Type Characters Want to Use Sports as a Vehicle to Push Their Own (Wacky) Politics. Don't Even Bother with Them." Twitter, January 17, 2023. https://twitter.com/Joe_in_NJ/status/1615565929739440128.

Chapter 5 – All-in on the Deception

In the first chapter, I outlined several infamous individuals who violated the tenets of journalism. These people, like Cooke, Blair, and Glass, by all accounts, appeared to operate independently from their bosses and employers. But in the last few years, there's been a shift in the landscape. Now it seems the alleged deceit is sanctioned by the media machines themselves.

The 1619 Project

Mainstream media succumbing to political and social narratives while covering issues and events is reprehensible; equally deserving of rebuke is when its members actively craft material with an agenda, in the attempt to rewrite history.

The 1619 Project, a multimedia initiative by *The New York Times*, which included a *New York Times Magazine* special, an online version, a book, and a series on Hulu, elicited both sweeping praise, including a Pulitzer Prize for founder and lead writer Nikole Hannah-Jones, as well as harsh criticism upon its release. As the dust has settled, it appears the project may have caused harm to the *Times*' credibility, although precisely how much is debatable.[1]

Published in 2019, the project postulated that an event 400 years ago – the arrival of the first slave ship on U.S. shores in 1619 – should now be considered the moment the nation was founded, not July 4, 1776. It then presented essays by various writers of how the vestiges of slavery have reverberated through social, political, and economic systems in America.[2]

After initial publication, the project was itself reframed by *The New York Times* and Hannah-Jones herself. According to Becket Adams of *The Washington Examiner*, the online version originally contained a phrase about the slave ship's landing as "understanding 1619 as our true founding" but was later removed.[3] In addition, Hannah-Jones uploaded a banner on her X profile that had the date July 4, 1776, crossed out in favor of August 20, 1619.[4]

In another *Washington Examiner* piece in 2020, Adams reports that Hannah-Jones admitted the project erred when she posited that "one of the primary reasons" for the Revolutionary War was to ensure that slavery continued. She later stated the correct wording should have read that "some of" the colonists, not all, were motivated to fight British rule to preserve slavery.[5]

Northwestern University history professor Leslie M. Harris maintains slavery had very little to do with why the colonists waged war against the British. In a Politico article, Harris talks of an interaction she had with Hannah-Jones and how her historical corrections were rejected.[6]

"At one point, she (Hannah-Jones) sent me this assertion: 'One critical reason that the colonists declared their independence from Britain was because they wanted to protect the institution of slavery in the colonies, which had produced tremendous wealth. At the time there were growing calls to abolish slavery throughout the British Empire, which would have badly damaged the economies of colonies in both North and South.' I vigorously disputed the claim. Although slavery was certainly an issue in the American Revolution, the protection of slavery was not one of the main reasons the 13 Colonies went to war."[7]

Harris was not the only scholar to take exception to the 1619 Project's troubling proclamations. On Dec. 4, 2019, five historians penned a letter to the *Times* expressing concerns over what they deemed "factual errors" in the project. Those errors included Harris' correction about the colonists' motivation for the American Revolution, and also important historical facts omitted from the project, such as Abraham Lincoln and Frederick Douglass agreeing that the U.S. Constitution was a "glorious liberty document."[8]

On Dec. 30, 2019, a second group of historians sent a letter to *The New York Times Magazine* expressing their deep reservations about the project. The magazine dismissed their concerns and did not issue any corrections.[9] The next year, they were followed by an even larger contingent of history professors, led by Peter Wood, president of the National Association of Scholars, who submitted a letter to the Pulitzer Prize Board, requesting that it revoke the prize awarded to Hannah-Jones for the 1619 Project. That didn't happen either.[10]

So, the big question is how history will treat the 1619 Project. The first page of an online search yields links to the project itself, its Pulitzer Prize, but also stories critical of the project. Indeed, the 1619 Project is forever marred by its controversies – what it got wrong and what it left out – but it displayed tremendous promise. There is no doubt slavery was a horrific chapter in America's history that should never be forgotten and deserves to be chronicled accurately. Unfortunately, the project was misguided from the start, beginning with its title, as the prospect of imposing a sweeping and frankly, fraudulent change to our nation's history proved to be insurmountable.

In addition to historical inaccuracies, many of the essays exhibited a sense of bitterness and negativity. One editorial strategy might have been to acknowledge the history in an accurate manner and then move the narrative forward in a more positive light. Yes, slavery was an absolute abomination, and no, America is not perfect, but how have things improved since then, and how can they in the future?

"Peaceful protests"

There's an iconic scene from the long-running Comedy Central show *South Park* in 1997, when Officer Barbrady frantically pulls up to a crime scene, media cameras in his face, and shouts, "Okay people, move along. There's nothing to see here."[11]

Sound familiar? The mainstream media engaged in the full gamut of journalistic gymnastics when they tried to downplay or outright misrepresent the carnage caused during riots across the country following the death of George Floyd in May of 2020.[12]

I believe there was a perceived obligation by the mainstream media to present the riots in that way – as insane as it appeared – for fear of reprisal from outside interests. Shame on them for that; that was not journalism. A media outlet cannot operate out of trepidation; to the contrary, it must operate with freedom and fearlessness. The type of behavior the mainstream media exhibited in its coverage of the riots is indicative of an entity that is beholden to someone, or several someones. When a newspaper or network has no fear, and no masters, it serves its viewers or readers with integrity and objectivity, precisely what it was designed to do.

In one of the most clear-cut examples, the media seemed to grapple with how to appear factual but also push an agenda as evidenced by a USNews.com headline, which read "George Floyd Protests Mostly Peaceful as Arrests Top 10,000."[13]

One CNN segment, reported by Brynn Gingras, illustrated cognitive dissonance at its best, with a chyron that read, "Peaceful protesters defy curfews, no widespread looting," but footage in the segment displayed looters breaking store windows, with one thug launching a bike through some plate glass. Oh, and there was "some tension" between the NYPD and protesters... to the tune of 200 arrests.[14]

In another CNN segment, a chyron read: "Fiery but mostly peaceful protests after police shooting," as reporter Omar Jiminez stood in front of a raging inferno and attempted to justify the carnage with, "What you are seeing, the common theme that ties all of this together is an expression of anger and frustration over what people feel like has become an all-too-familiar story playing out in places from across the country, not just here in Kenosha, Wisconsin."[15]

The subsequent "Mostly peaceful" memes were glorious: Jiminez photoshopped in front of the Chernobyl nuclear meltdown, JFK's assassination, and the Hindenburg explosion.[16]

Here is a headline from a YouTube video posted by the CBS Evening News: "Peaceful protesters continue to clash with federal agents in Portland." When anchor Norah O'Donnell introduces the segment, the phrase "Violent Protests" is seen in bold letters on the screen, but correspondent Carter Evans says "Peaceful protests turned violent." Let's be honest – when you have hordes of people packed into city streets and they are angry about something and see no other alternative but to destroy property and waylay the weak or those wearing uniforms, that's not peaceful. It's just a powder keg waiting to detonate. God forbid the media call them what they actually are – rioting rioters who riot.[17]

In perhaps the swiftest example of karma, CNN reporter Miguel Marquez was verbally accosted, and a bottle, along with another object, were hurled at him as he stood by a street, describing passing carloads of protesters as a "merry caravan."[18]

The Laptop from Hell

Arguably one of the most heinous acts committed by the media in recent memory was what appeared to be a concerted effort to conceal the information contained within a laptop belonging to Hunter Biden – or, as some have referred to it, the Laptop from Hell – just before the Presidential election of 2020.[19] Donald Trump popularized the phrase Laptop from Hell, not only for the lurid photos and videos of Hunter Biden's sexual debauchery with numerous prostitutes and rampant use of crack cocaine, but more importantly, for the alleged treasonous actions, specifically influence-peddling, by Hunter's father, then vice-President Joe Biden.[20]

The New York Post researched and published several exclusive stories on the laptop, beginning in October 2020. No other mainstream media outlets reciprocated in what, in some Americans' eyes, was quite possibly a presidential controversy that at least equaled, if not eclipsed the Watergate Scandal. One of the *Post*'s stories, dated Oct. 14, 2020, written by Emma-Jo Morris and Gabrielle Fonrouge, presents evidence that Biden allegedly used his position to coerce Ukrainian government officials into sacking a prosecutor who was leading a probe of Burisma, a Ukrainian energy company that employed Hunter Biden.[21]

According to a *New York Post* story by Steven Nelson on Nov. 21, 2022, it took CBS 769 days to report on the laptop. As a major news source, that is utterly embarrassing. The *Post* said other prominent news outlets like *The Washington Post* and *The New York Times* were still late to the party, but preceded CBS, first reporting on the laptop in March, which is still quite shameful.[22]

Mainstream media justified their disregard for the laptop by seizing on the opinion of 50 U.S. intelligence officials who wrote in a letter dated Oct. 19, 2020, that the laptop "has all the classic earmarks of a Russian information operation," although also admitting that they "do not have evidence of Russian involvement."[23]

Both Twitter and Facebook banned posts and links to the *Post*'s laptop story, according to The Verge, quoting a Twitter spokesperson who said, "In line with our hacked materials Policy, as well as our approach to blocking URLs, we are taking action to block any links to or images of the material in question on Twitter."[24] The problem was there was *the belief* that the laptop had been hacked – but it had not been proven. In actuality, the word "hacked" had been weaponized against Rudy Guiliani's procurement of the laptop and also to describe the laptop's material itself as "Russian disinformation." Both of which were later proven to be false.[25]

The story of the Laptop from Hell begins in 2019, when a man who identified himself as Hunter Biden dropped off a laptop at a Delaware computer repair store owned and operated by John Paul Mac Isaac, but never returned to reclaim it. After looking at the files and emails on the laptop, Mac Isaac turned it over to former New York City Mayor Rudy Guiliani, who at the time was the personal attorney for then-incumbent President Donald Trump.[26]

The laptop contained an April 17, 2015, email to Hunter Biden by Vadym Pozharskyi, an adviser to the board of Burisma, a Ukrainian energy company that, a year earlier, appointed Hunter Biden to its board on a reported salary of up to $50,000 a month, according to the *Post*.

> "'Dear Hunter, thank you for inviting me to DC and giving an opportunity to meet your father and spent [sic] some time together. It's realty [sic] an honor and pleasure,' the email reads, according to The Post. An earlier email from May 2014 also shows Pozharskyi,

reportedly Burisma's No. 3 exec, asking Hunter for "advice on how you could use your influence" on the company's behalf."[27]

This exposed the hypocrisy of Joe Biden's claim that he had "never spoken to my son about his overseas business dealings."[28]

"The laptop links President Biden to his son Hunter and brother Jim Biden's foreign influence-peddling, but high-ranking former spy agency officials claimed before the 2020 election it was likely Russian disinformation and the story was censored by Twitter and Facebook," *The New York Post*'s Steven Nelson wrote.[29]

In a column on April 12, 2022, in *The Wall Street Journal*, Holman W. Jenkins, Jr., states that "The job of 'newspapers of record' is to establish the truth or falsity of important matters in the public sphere, and whether the laptop was real or not certainly qualified."[30]

But, Jenkins states, there was an ulterior motive afoot to torpedo Donald Trump's re-election. "They'd seen this movie before – with James Comey's late intervention in 2016 – and 'knew' Donald Trump's re-election would be a disaster for the country."[31]

Even the liberal Bill Maher, host of HBO's *Real Time*, chose true journalism over fanatical partisanship, saying in 2022, "It looks like the left-wing media just buried the (Hunter Biden laptop) story because it wasn't part of their narrative and that's why people don't trust the media."[32]

And how about a reporter from an unnamed publication who adamantly refused to write anything negative about Hunter Biden? That's not journalism. Years before news of the laptop surfaced, there appears to have been behind-the-scenes suppression of potentially damaging information about Hunter

Biden's connection with Burisma, "dating back to 2015 when an aide to then-Vice President Joe Biden boasted she got a reporter to 'only use' negative information 'if her editors hold a gun to her head,'" according to a story on Justthenews.com.33

The Steele Dossier

In April 2016, attorney Marc Elias of Perkins Coie law firm hired a research group named Fusion GPS, which in turn hired British intelligence agent Christopher Steele to concoct a piece of opposition research on Republican Presidential nominee Donald Trump. Elias was representing both Democratic presidential nominee Hillary Clinton's campaign and the Democratic National Committee34 when he set the wheels in motion on what would eventually be known as the Steele dossier.

The dossier contained allegations about Trump's alleged sexual proclivities, but more importantly, made an attempt to connect him with the Kremlin and the notion that the two sides had conspired to win the 2016 Presidential election, according to a story on CNN.com written by Marshall Cohen.35

"But five years later, the credibility of the dossier has significantly diminished," Cohen writes. "A series of investigations and lawsuits have discredited many of its central allegations and exposed the unreliability of Steele's sources."36

So why did the media run with the dossier when it was unsubstantiated? According to Bill Grueskin, a professor at Columbia University's journalism school, it was Trump's "personality," according to a VOAnews.com story.37

"*Washington Post* fact-checkers would eventually catalog more than 30,000 Trump falsehoods during his term in the White House," Grueskin wrote in a column for *The New York Times*. "When a well-known liar tells you that something is false, the instinct is to believe that it might well be true." Grueskin wrote.[38]

That Trump uncorked thousands of "falsehoods" and is a "well-known liar" is arguable. Consider that during his presidency, he took an aggressive stance against what he referred to as "fake news" and viewed the *Post* to be a part of that – after all, the paper kept a running tab on his "lies" which, at one point, numbered more than 30,000[39] – and also that he is a conservative and the WaPo's agenda leans heavily to the left.

Another point to argue is whether the Steele dossier triggered the Robert Mueller special counsel investigation, or if the wheels were already in motion and its release simply bolstered what was suspected. The bottom line is that after a nearly two-year investigation into allegations of coordination with Russia and obstruction of justice, Mueller found there was not sufficient evidence to indict Trump on either charge.[40]

Paul Roderick Gregory penned an article in *Forbes* titled "The Trump Dossier Is Fake – And Here Are the Reasons Why," but apparently, nobody listened to him.

"This story makes no sense," Gregory writes. "In 2011, when the courtship purportedly begins, Trump was a TV personality and beauty pageant impresario. Neither in the U.S. or Russia would anyone of authority anticipate that Trump would one day become the presidential candidate of a major U.S. political party, making him the target of Russian intelligence."[41]

Sure, some of the mainstream media retracted their stories, but the damage had been done, arguably more to their reputations than to Trump.

"*The Washington Post*, for example, removed and corrected sections from two articles published in 2017 and 2019, and removed a video that summarized an earlier article," according to VOAnews.com.[42]

Another repercussion was that members of the mainstream media, typically in league, instead began cannibalizing one another.

"Media critic Erik Wemple issued the harsh rebuke in a column on Friday, calling on CNN to correct its longstanding claim that its reporting had verified substantial portions of the 2016 dossier alleging Donald Trump conspired with Russia," according to an article on the dailymail.com. "Last week, a federal indictment alleged that Russian-born analyst Igor Danchenko, a key source for the Steele dossier, fabricated conversations with one source, and used a Democratic political operative as another."[43]

And how's this for prejudicial coverage?

"Wemple argued that CNN had provided breathless, splashy coverage of its alleged corroboration of the dossier, but only muted and grudging air time for the Danchenko indictment that seriously undermined the dossier's claims."[44]

CNN's story is still up (as of 9/2/2024), with no context or explainer at the top, although Cohen's story could be characterized as a low-key *mea culpa*.[45]

Sara Fischer of Axios called the media's pursuit of the Steele dossier "one of the most egregious journalistic errors in modern history, and the media's response to its own mistakes has so far been tepid." She praises the *Post* for admitting its mistakes in its coverage and then states, "Other outlets that gave the document outsized coverage have so far been less forthcoming," referring to CNN, MSNBC, Mother Jones, and *The Wall Street Journal*.[46]

Ray Epps

When you think of the central figures of the January 6, 2021, protest at the U.S. Capitol, undoubtedly, Jacob Chansley, also known as the "QAnon Shaman" comes to mind, with his red, white, and blue face paint, horned headdress, and American flag attached to what appeared to be a spear. Chansley, who entered the Capitol, pleaded guilty to obstruction of an official proceeding and was sentenced to 41 months in prison, but was discharged early for good behavior.47

The second was retired U.S. Marine Ray Epps, who, clad in desert camo and a red Trump hat and carrying a rucksack on his back, emerged as a polarizing character in the subsequent U.S. House of Representatives investigation. Epps can be seen in several locations near and on Capitol grounds on Jan. 5 and 6, 2021. First, on the night of Jan. 5, 2021, footage showed Epps having a conversation with vlogger Tim "Baked Alaska" Gionet. At one point, Epps states, "In fact, tomorrow, I don't even like to say it because I'll be arrested..."

"Well, let's not say it," says Gionet.

"I'll say it," Epps says. "We need to go *in* to the Capitol."48

Then, in another exchange, while among a throng of Trump supporters, the towering, burly Epps bellowed, "Tomorrow, we need to go into the Capitol... into the Capitol!" Many of those standing near him seemed incredulous at the concept. "What?" one said and then several retorted "No!" and then Epps added, "Peacefully," but Gionet began pointing at Epps and chanting, "Fed! Fed! Fed!" and many in the crowd joined in.49

On Jan. 6, Epps was seen standing in the street as Trump supporters walked in various directions, yelling again, "As soon as our president is done speaking, we are going to the Capitol, where our problems are, it's that direction," as he motions with his hand. "Please spread the word."50

At a police barricade on the east side of the Capitol, Epps was seen on the front line of the protesters as they gathered in front of a fence. He then whispered into the ear of protester Ryan

Samsel. As soon as Epps stepped away, Samsel, a Pennsylvania barber, along with several others, began shoving the barricade toward the police officers standing behind it.[51]

Samsel later told investigators that Epps told him, "Dude... Relax, the cops are doing their job," but in an interview with American Greatness, Samsel contradicted his testimony, saying Epps told him, "Don't pull. I've got people. We have to push through."[52]

Then there is the footage of Epps running past the barricades, going deeper onto Capitol property as seen in an interview with *60 Minutes*.[53]

On Jan. 8, Epps' photo, tagged as "Suspect #16," was among several others released by the FBI on a most wanted poster, asking the public for information for the pictured individuals for "Violence at the United States Capitol." According to Revolver.com, in less than three days, Epps was identified; however, about six months later, on July 1, between the hours of 3:37 A.M. and 5:55 P.M., "someone at the FBI quietly and stealthily purged every trace of Ray Epps from the Capitol Riots Most Wanted database," Revolver states. It appears that other suspects, despite their respective arrests, remained on the most wanted list, with a red band underneath their photos that read "Arrested."[54]

According to Epps' attorney, "The government initially declined to prosecute Epps in 2021 after the FBI investigated his conduct on Jan. 6 and found insufficient evidence to charge him with a crime, according to [Epps' attorney Edward] Ungvarsky. Epps isn't accused of entering the Capitol or engaging in any violence or destruction on Jan. 6."[55]

On Jan. 21, 2022, Epps was interviewed by the Select Committee to Investigate the January 6th Attack on the U.S. Capitol. When asked about his imperative to go into the Capitol, he claimed that he was not trying to incite violence, but curiously, attempting to prevent it.[56]

"The Capitol is the people's House, and the rotunda – people can go into the rotunda and – and see what's happening there. My vision was get as many people in there as we can and surround it, be there, let them know that we're not happy with the – with what – what has happened, and that was it. No violence."[57]

During his testimony, Epps also addressed the point at which he said he might get arrested, saying, "I don't know. It was the heat of the moment thing. I was trying to find some common ground with these people and change their minds. It shouldn't have been said, but I said it."[58]

Epps also said he had never worked for, nor communicated with, any law enforcement individuals or entities, either before or during the protests.[59]

As far as his interaction with Samsel at the barricades, Epps said that he had seen Samsel shaking the barrier, "And then I went out and talked to him and told him, Okay, you know, that's not why we're here. You've got to be peaceful, pulled him back and told him, It's not what we're about."[60]

Revolver's work on Ray Epps landed on the radar of *The New York Times* and was mentioned in a story on July 13, 2022. "Obscure right-wing media outlets, like Revolver News, used selectively edited videos and unfounded leaps of logic to paint him as a secret federal asset in charge of a 'breach team' responsible for setting off the riot at the Capitol."[61]

Revolver, in turn, panned the *Times*' story on Epps as a "puff piece" that omitted key elements of his alleged motivations and actions on Jan. 5 and 6.[62]

Epps states in the *Times* interview that the reason he avoided arrest was that he spoke with the FBI as soon as he found out he was wanted. "The interview transcripts show that Mr. Epps told agents that he had spent much of his time at the Capitol seeking to calm down other rioters, an assertion supported by multiple video clips."[63]

Here are some other alleged deficiencies in the *Times* story:

– The link to the "multiple video clips" shows one clip on Rumble of Epps walking in the space between protesters and police at the Capitol on Jan. 6, as he is attempting to calm down the protesters, saying to them, "Take a step back, we're going ground, we're not trying to get people hurt."[64]

– *The Times* did not appear to press Epps on why he moved past the barricade if he told Samsel not to do it. They didn't appear to ask him about the Jan. 6 clip where he directed people to go to the Capitol "where our problems are."[65]

– They didn't appear to ask him why he was part of a group moving a giant Trump flag[66] on Jan. 6, as seen briefly at 7:27 of the *60 Minutes* interview.[67] Prosecutor Michael Gordon said the sign was pushed "into a group of police officers," according to a story from the AP.[68]

– Calling Revolver "obscure" but then exposing them on a larger platform (their own) seems counter-intuitive.[69]

– The *Times* appeared to frame the situation stating, "But through a series of events that twisted his role, he became the face of this conspiracy theory about the F.B.I. as it spread from the fringes to the mainstream." It is not for the *Times* to say the events "twisted his role." Allow Epps to say it and allow readers to reach that conclusion, if they choose to do so.[70]

– "But scores, if not hundreds, of people who appear to have committed minor crimes that day were investigated by the

F.B.I. but have not been charged or taken into custody." Where is the source for this?[71]

— It doesn't appear that they pressed Epps on whether or not he was allegedly acting as an asset of the federal government.[72]

A *New York Times* story on Jan. 9, 2024, which discussed Epps' sentence of a year of probation, said he played a "small role" in the protests. Prosecutors had requested he serve six months in prison, according to the story. The year before, Epps pleaded guilty to one count of disorderly conduct.[73]

Epps' sentence marked the end of his adjudication, "But it was unlikely to end the persistent false narrative that he was a provocateur out to entrap his fellow conservatives on Jan. 6 even though he, his lawyer, the prosecutor, and even the judge overseeing the case all asserted in open court that the tale was preposterous."[74]

---

[1] Tombleson, Rodney John. "1619 Project Has No Credibility." Rodney John Tombleson Blog, February 1, 2021. https://tombleson.us/2021/02/1619-project-has-no-credibility/.

[2] Kaufman, Elliot. "The '1619 Project' Gets Schooled." Opinion, December 16, 2019. https://www.wsj.com/articles/the-1619-project-gets-schooled-11576540494.

[3] Adams, Becket. "The 1619 Project Is a Fraud." *Washington Examiner*, September 21, 2020. https://www.washingtonexaminer.com/opinion/688398/the-1619-project-is-a-fraud/.

[4] Ibid.

[5] Adams, Becket. "Seven Months Later, 1619 Project Leader Admits She Got It Wrong." *Washington Examiner*, March 13, 2020. https://www.washingtonexaminer.com/opinion/1725211/seven-months-later-1619-project-leader-admits-she-got-it-wrong/.

[6] Harris, Leslie M. "I helped fact-check the 1619 project. The Times Ignored Me." Politico, March 6, 2020. https://www.politico.com/news/magazine/2020/03/06/1619-project-new-york-times-mistake-122248.

7 Ibid.

8 "We Respond to the Historians Who Critiqued the 1619 Project." *The New York Times*, December 20, 2019.
https://www.nytimes.com/2019/12/20/magazine/we-respond-to-the-historians-who-critiqued-the-1619-project.html.

9 "Twelve Scholars Critique the 1619 Project and the *New York Times Magazine* Editor Responds." History News Network, January 26, 2020.
https://hnn.us/article/twelve-scholars-critique-the-1619-project-and-the-.

10 Wood, Peter. "Pulitzer Board Must Revoke Nikole Hannah-Jones' Prize by Peter Wood." National Association of Scholars, October 6, 2020.
https://www.nas.org/blogs/article/pulitzer-board-must-revoke-nikole-hannah-jones-prize.

11 Miami Bad Boy BOSS. "Nothing to See Here." YouTube, February 2, 2014. https://www.youtube.com/watch?v=LW6RWSiR88s.

12 Krakauer, Steve. "The Media Is Ignoring the Violence That's Tearing Our Cities Apart." The Hill, August 19, 2020.
https://thehill.com/opinion/criminal-justice/512622-the-media-is-ignoring-the-violence-thats-tearing-our-cities-apart/.

13 Smith-Schoenwalder, Cecelia. "George Floyd Protests Mostly Peaceful as Arrests Top 10,000." *US News & World Report*, June 4, 2020.
https://www.usnews.com/news/national-news/articles/2020-06-04/george-floyd-protests-mostly-peaceful-as-arrests-top-10-000.

14 Gingras, Brynn. "Peaceful Protests across Much of US despite Breaking Curfew." CNN, June 3, 2020.
https://www.cnn.com/videos/us/2020/06/03/peaceful-protests-across-us-floyd-gingras-newday-pkg-vpx.cnn.

15 Lancaster, Jordan. "CNN Chyron Calls Wisconsin Riots 'Mostly Peaceful' as Correspondent Stands in Front of a Burning Building." The Daily Caller, August 27, 2020. https://dailycaller.com/2020/08/27/cnn-chiron-wisconsin-riots-mostly-peaceful-correspondent-burning-building/.

16 "Omar+Jimenez+mostly+peaceful+memes." Yahoo! Accessed March 31, 2024.
https://images.search.yahoo.com/search/images;_ylt=AwrJ.PMLn_9lBgQAAdNXNyoA;_ylu=Y29sbwNiZjEEcG9zAzEEdnRpZAMEc2VjA3BpdnM-?p=omar%2Bjimenez%2Bmostly%2Bpeaceful%2Bmemes&fr2=piv-web&type=E210US105G91826&fr=mcafee&guccounter=1.

17 CBS Evening News. "Peaceful Protesters Continue to Clash with Federal Agents in Portland." YouTube, July 27, 2020.
https://www.youtube.com/watch?v=wLLtYAP5TGE.

18 DailyWire+. "Media's 'Peaceful Protest' Narrative Shatters on Live TV." YouTube, June 1, 2020. https://www.youtube.com/watch?v=_sJZbKDy-Fk.

19 Tobin, Jonathan. "Burying the Hunter Biden Laptop Story Was Journalistic Malpractice." *Newsweek*, March 25, 2022. https://www.newsweek.com/burying-hunter-biden-laptop-story-was-journalistic-malpractice-opinion-1691437.

20 Deese, Kaelan. "Trump Claims He's Seen Hunter Biden's 'Laptop from Hell,' Makes Al Capone Look like a Baby." *Washington Examiner*, July 7, 2021. https://www.washingtonexaminer.com/news/1473745/trump-claims-hes-seen-hunter-bidens-laptop-from-hell-makes-al-capone-look-like-a-baby/.

21 Morris, Emma-Jo, and Gabrielle Fonrouge. "Smoking-Gun Email Reveals How Hunter Biden Introduced Ukrainian Businessman to VP Dad." *New York Post*, October 14, 2020. https://nypost.com/2020/10/14/email-reveals-how-hunter-biden-introduced-ukrainian-biz-man-to-dad/.

22 Nelson, Steven. "CBS 'Confirms' Hunter Biden Laptop Is Real 769 Days After Post Broke Story." *New York Post*, November 21, 2022. https://nypost.com/2022/11/21/cbs-confirms-hunter-biden-laptop-is-real-769-days-after-post-broke-story/.

23 "Public Statement on the Hunter Biden Emails." Politico. October 19, 2020. https://www.politico.com/f/?id=00000175-4393-d7aa-af77-579f9b330000.

24 Robertson, Adi. "Facebook and Twitter Are Restricting a Disputed *New York Post* Story about Joe Biden's Son." The Verge, October 14, 2020. https://www.theverge.com/2020/10/14/21515972/facebook-new-york-post-hunter-biden-story-fact-checking-reduced-distribution-election-misinformation.

25 McCarthy, Andrew C. "Hunter Biden Digs Hole Even Deeper by Falsely Claiming Laptop Was 'Hacked.'" *New York Post*, September 26, 2023. https://nypost.com/2023/09/26/hunter-biden-digs-hole-even-deeper-by-falsely-claiming-laptop-was-hacked/.

26 Cleary, Tom. "John Paul Mac Isaac: Store Owner in Hunter Biden *New York Post* Story Identified." Heavy.com, Updated August 25, 2023. https://heavy.com/news/john-paul-mac-isaac/.

27 Morris, Emma-Jo, and Gabrielle Fonrouge. "Smoking-Gun Email Reveals How Hunter Biden Introduced Ukrainian Businessman to VP Dad." *New York Post*, October 14, 2020. https://nypost.com/2020/10/14/email-reveals-how-hunter-biden-introduced-ukrainian-biz-man-to-dad/.

28 Baragona, Justin. "Joe Biden: 'I've Never Spoken to My Son About' Ukraine Business Deals." The Daily Beast, September 21, 2019. https://www.thedailybeast.com/joe-biden-ive-never-spoken-to-my-son-about-ukraine-business-deals.

29 Nelson, Steven. "CBS 'Confirms' Hunter Biden Laptop Is Real 769 Days After Post Broke Story." *New York Post*, November 21, 2022. https://nypost.com/2022/11/21/cbs-confirms-hunter-biden-laptop-is-real-769-days-after-post-broke-story/.

30 Jenkins, Holman Jr. "Media Bias and Hunter's Laptop," WSJ.com, April 12, 2022. https://www.wsj.com/articles/media-spin-hunter-biden-laptop-news-trump-free-speech-censorship-stop-the-steal-big-lie-2020-presidential-election-steele-dossier-11649792758.

31 Jenkins Jr., Holman W. "Media Bias and Hunter's Laptop." *Wall Street Journal*, Opinion, April 12, 2022. https://www.wsj.com/articles/media-spin-hunter-biden-laptop-news-trump-free-speech-censorship-stop-the-steal-big-lie-2020-presidential-election-steele-dossier-11649792758.

32 Wulfsohn, Joseph A. "Bill Maher: The 'Left-Wing Media' Buried the Hunter Biden Scandal Because 'It Wasn't Part of Their Narrative.'" Fox News, April 2, 2022. https://www.foxnews.com/media/bill-maher-hunter-biden-left-wing-media.

33 Hazard, Charlotte, and John Solomon. "Effort to Squash Biden Family Stories Long Predated Hunter Laptop, Newly Released Emails Reveal." Just The News, March 23, 2023. https://justthenews.com/accountability/political-ethics/new-memos-government-effort-suppress-biden-family-stories-began.

34 Entous, Adam, et al. "Clinton Campaign, DNC Helped Fund Research." *The Columbus Dispatch*, October 25, 2017. https://www.dispatch.com/story/news/politics/elections/national/2017/10/25/clinton-campaign-dnc-helped-fund/17942952007/.

35 Cohen, Marshall. "The Steele Dossier: A Reckoning." CNN, November 18, 2021. https://www.cnn.com/2021/11/18/politics/steele-dossier-reckoning/index.html.

36 Ibid.

37 Gorbachev, Alexey. "Discredited 'Steele Dossier' Flags Important Lessons for Media." Voice of America, December 7, 2021. https://www.VOAnews.com/a/discredited-steele-dossier-flags-important-lessons-for-media/6342968.html.

38 Ibid.

39 Choi, Joseph. "*Washington Post* Counts 30,573 False or Misleading Claims in Four Years by Trump." The Hill, January 20, 2021.

https://thehill.com/homenews/media/535081-wapost-counts-30573-false-or-misleading-claims-in-four-years-by-trump/.

40 "Mueller Finds No Collusion with Russia, Leaves Obstruction Question Open." American Bar Association, March 25, 2019. https://www.americanbar.org/news/abanews/aba-news-archives/2019/03/mueller-concludes-investigation/.

41 Gregory, Paul Roderick. "The Trump Dossier Is Fake – and Here Are the Reasons Why." *Forbes*, January 13, 2017. https://www.forbes.com/sites/paulroderickgregory/2017/01/13/the-trump-dossier-is-false-news-and-heres-why/?sh=7950c78e6867.

42 Gorbachev, Alexey. "Discredited 'Steele Dossier' Flags Important Lessons for Media." Voice of America, December 7, 2021. https://www.voanews.com/a/discredited-steele-dossier-flags-important-lessons-for-media/6342968.html.

43 Griffith, Keith. "*Washington Post* Columnist Demands CNN Retract Claim That Steele Dossier Had Been 'Partly Corroborated' After Key Source Was Arrested for Lying – As Paper Corrects Its Own Stories." Daily Mail Online, November 12, 2021. https://www.dailymail.co.uk/news/article-10196961/Washington-Post-columnist-demands-CNN-retract-corroboration-claim-Steele-dossier.html.

44 Ibid.

45 Sciutto, Jim, and Evan Perez. "US Investigators Corroborate Some Aspects of the Russia Dossier." CNN, February 10, 2017. https://www.cnn.com/2017/02/10/politics/russia-dossier-update/index.html.

46 Fischer, Sara. "The Media's Epic Fail on the Steele Dossier." Axios, November 14, 2021. https://www.axios.com/2021/11/14/steele-dossier-discredited-media-corrections-buzzfeed-washington-post.

47 Kim, Juliana. "U.S. Capitol Rioter the 'QAnon Shaman' Is Released Early from Federal Prison." NPR, March 31, 2023. https://www.npr.org/2023/03/31/1167319814/qanon-shaman-jacob-chansley-capitol-riot-early-release-reentry.

48 "Ray Epps – Same Routine, Again and Again." Rumble, accessed March 31, 2024. https://rumble.com/vo7hj1-ray-epps-same-routine-again-and-again.html.

49 Isaacson, Tom. "Ray Epps Shouted Down by Crowd as a Fed – Jan 5 Jan 6." YouTube, January 11, 2022. https://www.youtube.com/watch?v=erafzh-YahE.

50 "Ray Epps – As Soon as Our President Is Done Speaking." Rumble, accessed March 31, 2024. https://rumble.com/vo7ibv-ray-epps-as-soon-as-our-president-is-done-speaking.html.

51 "Ray Epps – the Moment the 1/6 Police Barricades Were First Stormed." Rumble, accessed March 31, 2024. https://rumble.com/vo7igb-ray-epps-the-moment-the-16-police-barricades-were-first-stormed.html.

52 Kelly, Julie. "J6 Defendant on Ray Epps: 'They Are Protecting Him Like Crazy' ' American Greatness." American Greatness, June 7, 2023. https://amgreatness.com/2023/06/07/j6-defendant-on-ray-epps-they-are-protecting-him-like-crazy/.

53 "Ray Epps: The *60 Minutes* Interview." YouTube, 60 Minutes, April 24, 2023. https://www.youtube.com/watch?v=QHEEGxQKg20.

54 "Meet Ray Epps: The Fed-Protected Provocateur Who Appears to Have Led the Very First 1/6 Attack on the US Capitol." Revolver News, October 25, 2021. https://revolver.news/2021/10/meet-ray-epps-the-fed-protected-provocateur-who-appears-to-have-led-the-very-first-1-6-attack-on-the-u-s-capitol/.

55 Kunzelman, Michael. "Ray Epps, a Target of Jan. 6 Conspiracy Theories, Gets a Year of Probation for His Capitol Riot Role." AP News, January 9, 2024. https://apnews.com/article/ray-epps-conspiracy-theory-capitol-riot-fbbfca2fc1c13c439fca7d460237934c.

56 U.S. House of Representatives. "Select committee to investigate the 6 January 6th attack ..." January 21, 2022. https://www.govinfo.gov/content/pkg/GPO-J6-TRANSCRIPT-CTRL0000038864/pdf/GPO-J6-TRANSCRIPT-CTRL0000038864.pdf.

57 Ibid.

58 Ibid.

59 Ibid.

60 Ibid.

61 Feuer, Alan. "A Trump Backer's Downfall as the Target of a Jan. 6 Conspiracy Theory." *The New York Times*, July 13, 2022. https://www.nytimes.com/2022/07/13/us/politics/jan-6-conspiracy-theory-ray-epps.html.

62 "The Hidden Agenda Behind the *New York Times*' Desperate Puff Piece on Ray Epps." Revolver.com, July 14, 2022. https://revolver.news/2022/07/the-hidden-agenda-behind-new-york-times-desperate-ray-epps-puff-piece/.

63 Ibid.

64 "Ray Epps – Holding Court at Front of Police Line." Rumble, accessed March 31, 2024. https://rumble.com/vo7gs1-ray-epps-holding-court-at-front-of-police-line.html.

65 Ibid.

66 Ibid.

67 "Ray Epps: The *60 Minutes* Interview." YouTube, 60 Minutes, April 24, 2023. https://www.youtube.com/watch?v=QHEEGxQKg2o.

68 Kunzelman, Michael. "Ray Epps, a Target of Jan. 6 Conspiracy Theories, Gets a Year of Probation for His Capitol Riot Role." AP News, January 9, 2024. https://apnews.com/article/ray-epps-conspiracy-theory-capitol-riot-fbbfca2fc1c13c439fca7d460237934c.

69 Feuer, Alan. "A Trump Backer's Downfall as the Target of a Jan. 6 Conspiracy Theory." *The New York Times*, July 13, 2022. https://www.nytimes.com/2022/07/13/us/politics/jan-6-conspiracy-theory-ray-epps.html.

70 Ibid.

71 Ibid.

72 Ibid.

73 Montague, Zach, and Alan Feuer. "Ray Epps, Target of Jan. 6 Conspiracy Theory, Is Sentenced to Probation." *The New York Times*, January 9, 2024. https://www.nytimes.com/2024/01/09/us/politics/ray-epps-sentenced-january-6.html.

74 Ibid.

Chapter 6 – Fact-checking Is Unnecessary

"Who fact-checks the fact-checkers?" —Ted Czech

Snopes.com purports itself to be "The definitive fact-checking site," but boy oh boy, was there a staffer gaffe in January 2024. At that time, President Biden traveled to Superior, Wisconsin, and participated in a photo-op with a group of construction workers. Some genius had the great idea to put hard-workin' Joe in a hard hat, which none of the other people in the pic were wearing. This resulted in utter ridicule because the hat was on backwards, with the band and tightening knob on Biden's forehead. Pretty much everybody – except for Biden's handlers and Snopes, it seems – knows the band and tightening knob go in the back. After all, the tightening knob apparatus is also called a "nape strap" and well, the nape is the rear of a person's neck. Snopes then swooped in and posted that the claim that Biden wore the hat backwards was false. After the entire internet guffawed at Snopes and flooded them with criticism, they changed their ruling to true, grumbling about how the brim was facing forward.[1]

Here's what some X users had to say after the Snopes debacle:

> The Raymond G Stanley Jr @raymondgstanley: "It's clear that the male feminists who work at @snopes never wore a hard hat in their lives."[2]

> Ian McKelvey @ian_mckelvey: "Leftist white collar elites at Snopes trying to figure out how hard hats work. Understandable given that they routinely shit on the

middle class to run cover for the Democratic Party's exploitation efforts."[3]

End Wokeness @EndWokeness: Snopes fact-check: "Biden wore a hard hat backwards" is misinformation. Who are you going to believe: Snopes or your lying eyes?[4]

Months later, Snopes stepped into it again in early March 2024 over a controversy about the banning of the famous V-J Day kiss in a New York City photo.[5]

Dredging up memories of those who think that "Baby, It's Cold Outside" is some kind of bizarre screed of misogynistic-patriarchy-domestic violence, a memo from RimaAnn Nelson, the U.S. Department of Veterans Affairs assistant secretary for health for operations, requested the photo be removed from all VA facilities because it "depicts a non-consensual act" which is "inconsistent with the VA's no-tolerance policy towards sexual harassment and assault."[6]

Snopes swung into action, saying it was a false claim that the VA banned the photo. In the same story, Snopes admits the memo "is not, in fact, a fabrication," but "its distribution was made in error."[7]

Back to the phrase under the title of this chapter, "Who fact-checks the fact-checkers," it's one I uncorked during a morning Teams meeting at the newspaper, sometime in the thick of the pandemic. We were all in our respective homes, despite the newsroom enduring an "extra deep cleaning" according to the editor. I'm not sure if I was the first to ever utter the phrase, but I can tell you my inspiration was from the DC movie *The Watchmen*, where the question, "Who watches the watchmen?" is presented. In the film, society had turned on its protectors, the superheroes, when it realized they were all-powerful but that no checks-and-balances were in place.[8] So if you have a group that has declared itself an authority on something, who is making sure *they* are legitimate? If I recall correctly, the response from a coworker to my utterance was to dismiss me as being a nihilist.

Within the past decade or so – with a serious ramping up the last few years – the concepts of "fact-checking" and "mis-, dis- and malinformation" have been infused into American culture. I'm here to dismiss these ideas as what I call junk journalism. They have no business being associated with true journalism and only serve as vehicles to quickly and ultimately discredit oppositional thinking. George Orwell, were he still alive, would be shaking his damn head because we have finally reached the point where his idea of wrongthink – "beliefs or opinions that run contrary to the prevailing or mainstream orthodoxy" – has come to fruition.[9]

As mentioned in Chapter 3, as journalists, we accept the task of providing both or all sides of a story and then leaving it up to the audience to decide what they believe. That's the true beauty of American journalism; it fosters critical thinking.

The practice of fact-checking is puzzling, and frankly, a superfluous creation. Why would we need to separate fact-checking from journalism? Isn't that what reporters should be doing anyway? Fact-checking should be baked-in to the product of journalism. But as I looked at a few examples, it became clear that news outlets weren't fact-checking themselves – no, why would they do a thing like that – but instead were examining other pieces of news that were floating in the media ether. But what if the facts that the fact-checkers were presenting to counter the incorrect facts were in fact, incorrect? Now we've got a really big problem on our hands.

Digging deeper, it appears these fact-checking outfits have an anti-conservative agenda. *The New York Post* editorial board described fact-checking as "serving as a cover for partisan, left-wing opinion."[10] An overwhelming majority of the content on CNN's fact-check webpage concerns Donald Trump and other figures in the Republican party, but mainly Trump. My theory is it's because Trump *is* money; even though CNN and other left-leaning networks clearly detest him, they can't help but cover him constantly because they know he generates attention.[11]

A 2013 study conducted by Dr. Robert S. Lichter, head of the Center for Media and Public Affairs, examined PolitiFact.org, a fact-checking website owned by the Poynter Institute, and concluded that the website found Republicans to be less credible by a ratio of 3 to 1 compared to Democrats. However, the reasons behind these results have very little to do with facts and more to do with internal biases, according to *US News and World Report*'s Peter Roff.[12]

A 2020 story from *Scientific American* sums it up thusly: "Journalists and fact-checkers are human beings subject to the same psychological biases as everyone else – and their analyses of what constitute 'facts' is affected by their own political and ideological values, resulting in what psychologists term selective perception."[13]

The *SA* article continues: "When it comes to partisan fact-checking about complex issues – which describes much of the fact-checking that takes place in the context of political news – the truth as stated is often the subjective opinion of people with shared political views."[14]

One result of fact-checking, it seems, is that it has sown another layer of distrust of the media by the American public. In a 2018 poynter.org story titled "Fact-checkers are no longer a fresh-faced movement. They're fighting for the future of the internet," the fact-checking "industry" turned a bit introspective, seemingly doubting the point of its existence.[15]

"A dark cloud hangs over us. The disaffection and distrust that have plagued mainstream media outlets for many years is now spilling over to fact-checkers," said International Fact-Checking Network Director Alexios Mantazarlis at the fifth annual Global Fact-Checking Summit.[16]

About four years later, the climate for fact-checking evolved into a situation far more grave. Fact-checking, according to theconversation.com, may have contributed to the corrosion of the covenant between the media and its audience.

In the story, "Fact-checking can actually harm trust in media: New research," researchers Andrea Carson, Andrew Gibbons, Aaron Martin, and Justin B. Phillips requested 1,600 Australians to read a political news story and then half of them also read a fact-check about the story.[17]

"Concerningly, we found that when participants read the AAP fact check after reading the news story, trust in the original story fell sharply (by 13% overall), even after respondents' political or news source preferences were taken into account. Counter-intuitively, the act of fact-checking had a clear negative influence on readers' trust in the original news story."[18]

The caveat to all this is that "fact-checking" – at least on free-speech platforms like X – is a bit of a Frankenstein's monster, as the creature that was constructed as a weapon is turned on its creators. On Jan. 2, 2024, Harvard University President Claudine Gay resigned from her post amidst a firestorm of criticism for numerous counts of plagiarism over a period of years and the Harvard University Corporation for not terminating her. Gay initially caught the public's attention when she appeared before the House Committee on Education and the Workforce in December 2023 and failed to denounce threats calling for the genocide of Jews by Harvard student groups.[19] Gay resigned in January 2024, but instead of accepting responsibility for any of her alleged actions and inaction, she assumed the role of victim, saying she had been "subjected to personal attacks and threats fueled by racial animus."[20]

The Associated Press took up the mantle for Gay on Jan. 3, 2024, with a story titled "Plagiarism charges downed Harvard's president. A conservative attack helped to fan the outrage." But, according to the *Daily Mail*,[21] that was not the original headline; the first one for the story read, "Harvard president's resignation highlights new conservative weapon against colleges: plagiarism."[22]

According to the *Daily Mail*, the second headline was written after the AP was swiftly "fact-checked" into oblivion by other X users who wrote in community notes that accompanied the post, "Plagiarism is a breach of rules for Harvard University."[23]

It should be noted that the AP has a policy against plagiarism as well: "An AP staffer who reports and writes a story must use original content, language and phrasing. We do not plagiarize, meaning that we do not take the work of others and pass it off as our own."[24]

A *Vice* article, titled "Scientists Explain Why 'Doing Your Own Research' Leads to Believing Conspiracies," discusses the prospect of individuals using the internet to explore the veracity of an idea or issue after reading a story by the media.[25]

The challenge is that most people don't know how to use search engines properly, so the researchers say.[26]

> "Digital literacy curricula shouldn't just say to search, but instead offer advice on how to search, Kevin Aslett, an assistant professor at the University of Central Florida and co-author, told Motherboard. He and his fellow researchers suggest paying attention to the source of the information you're searching, not just the

content. Aslett added that more resources need to be pumped into fact-checking organizations so they can at least start to fill the data void that exists."[27]

But who determines which sources are credible and which are not? And since it's already been established that fact-checking entities are fallible, it may not be a wise decision to simply throw more money at them so they will pump out more questionable content.

---

[1] Emery, David. "Did Biden Wear a Hard Hat Backwards in Photo Op with Construction Workers?" Snopes, January 26, 2024. https://www.snopes.com/fact-check/biden-wear-hardhat-backwards/.

[2] @RaymondGStanley. "It's Clear That the Male Feminists Who Work at @Snopes Never Wore a Hard Hat in Their Lives." Twitter, January 27, 2024. https://twitter.com/search?q=%40raymondgstanley%20%40snopes%20&src=typed_query.

[3] McKelvey, Ian. "Leftist White Collar Elites at Snopes Trying to Figure out How Hard Hats Work." Twitter, January 27, 2024. https://twitter.com/ian_mckelvey/status/1751353339697049844.

[4] Emery, David. "Did Biden Wear a Hard Hat Backwards in Photo Op with Construction Workers?" Snopes, January 26, 2024. https://www.snopes.com/fact-check/biden-wear-hardhat-backwards/.

[5] @EndWokeness. "Snopes Fact-Check: 'Biden Wore a Hard Hat Backwards' Is Misinformation." Twitter, January 27, 2024. https://twitter.com/EndWokeness/status/1751310414460190937.

[6] Ibid.

[7] Ibid.

[8] Rotten Tomatoes Classic Trailer. "Watchmen (2009) Official Trailer - Zac Snyder Superhero Movie HD." YouTube, April 11, 2014. https://www.youtube.com/watch?v=wglmbroElUo.

[9] "Wrongthink." Wiktionary. Accessed March 31, 2024. https://en.wiktionary.org/wiki/wrongthink.

[10] *Post* Editorial Board. "Fact-Checking the Fact-Checkers: 'Pants on Fire' Partisans." *New York Post*, August 13, 2021. https://nypost.com/2021/08/13/fact-checking-the-fact-checkers-pants-on-fire-partisans/.

[11] Alberta, Tim. "Inside the Meltdown at CNN." *The Atlantic*, June 2, 2023. https://www.theatlantic.com/politics/archive/2023/06/cnn-ratings-chris-licht-trump/674255/.

[12] Roff, Peter. "Who's Checking the Fact Checkers?" *US News & World Report*, May 28, 2013. https://www.usnews.com/opinion/blogs/peter-roff/2013/05/28/study-finds-fact-checkers-biased-against-republicans.

[13] Ceci, Stephen J., and Wendy M. Williams. "The Psychology of Fact-Checking." *Scientific American*, October 25, 2020. https://www.scientificamerican.com/article/the-psychology-of-fact-checking1/.

[14] Ibid.

[15] Mantzarlis, Alexios. "Fact-Checkers Are No Longer a Fresh-Faced Movement. They're Fighting for the Future of the Internet." Poynter, June 20, 2018. https://www.poynter.org/fact-checking/2018/fact-checkers-are-no-longer-a-fresh-faced-movement-theyre-fighting-for-the-future-of-the-internet/.

[16] Ibid.

[17] Carson, Andrea, et al. "Fact-Checking Can Actually Harm Trust in Media: New Research." The Conversation, March 3, 2022. https://theconversation.com/fact-checking-can-actually-harm-trust-in-media-new-research-176032.

[18] Ibid.

[19] Davis, Jack. "Harvard Board Announces Decision on President Amid Anti-Semitism and Plagiarism Scandals." *The Western Journal*, Dec. 12, 2023. https://www.westernjournal.com/harvard-board-announces-decision-president-amid-anti-semitism-plagiarism-scandals/.

[20] Gay, Claudine. "Read Claudine Gay's resignation letter." *The New York Times*, Jan. 2, 2024. https://www.nytimes.com/2024/01/02/us/claudine-gay-resignation-letter-harvard.html.

[21] Richter, Emma. "Associated Press Is Forced into Humiliating U-Turn on Ousted Harvard President Claudine Gay Article After Sensational Headline That Claimed Academic Crime of Plagiarism Was a 'New Conservative Weapon.'" Daily Mail Online, January 3, 2024. https://www.dailymail.co.uk/news/article-12923691/associated-press-harvard-president-claudine-gay-conservative-weapon.html.

[22] Binkley, Collin, and Moriah Balingit. "Plagiarism Charges Downed Harvard's President. A Conservative Attack Helped to Fan the Outrage." AP News, January 3, 2024. https://apnews.com/article/harvard-president-plagiarism-claudine-gay-

3b048da1f2ee17b5edec3680b5828e8f?utm_campaign=TrueAnthem&utm_medium=AP&utm_source=Twitter.

23 Harvard University. "Harvard University Plagiarism Policy." Harvard Guide to Using Sources, accessed March 31, 2024. https://usingsources.fas.harvard.edu/harvard-plagiarism-policy.

24 The Associated Press. "Telling the Story." AP, February 7, 2024. https://www.ap.org/about/news-values-and-principles/telling-the-story/#:~:text=An%20AP%20staffer%20who%20reports,it%20off%20as%20our%20own.

25 Guesgen, Mirjam. "Scientists Explain Why 'Doing Your Own Research' Leads to Believing Conspiracies." *Vice*, December 21, 2023. https://www.vice.com/en/article/v7bjpm/scientists-explain-why-doing-your-own-research-leads-to-buying-conspiracies.

26 Ibid.

27 Ibid.

PART 2

FALLOUT

Chapter 7 – Donald Trump

It had to end.

With all that transpired in the first section – including the hoaxes, the rise of technology, and sensationalism, along with a concerted effort in college curriculums to disregard objectivity in favor of activism – it's no wonder the American public rejected the mass media en masse.

And so, the de facto anti-mainstream media movement, which intensified as consumers became increasingly frustrated and distrustful, installed its titular head, or in this case, two – Donald Trump and Elon Musk.

You may detest Trump as an individual – maybe you're turned off by his brash and arrogant personality – but what is undeniable is that never in modern history has an American president adopted a pugilistic style of interacting with the media, unleashing a fusillade of punches that set it reeling on its back foot. And maybe, just maybe, that's what the media needed.

Trump never relented, because it is his essence. He took his pugnacious, ego-driven, New York tycoon-style of conducting business and applied it to the presidency. But as much as the media detested Trump, they found covering him irresistible. As I said in Chapter 6, the media financially benefited from the adversarial relationship; reporting on Trump meant increased ratings. Since Trump left office, ratings for his biggest opponents, who ran overwhelmingly negative stories about him day-in and day-out, tanked.

"Two years of Donald Trump as president has been very good for their journalism, and even better for their company bottom lines," according to a *Forbes* story written by David Bloom in 2017. "CNN, now part of the AT&T megalith, just reported $1.5 billion in profits on a mere $2.3 billion in revenue, despite Trump's repeated complaints about its coverage of his administration, and repeated disparaging comments about its ratings ... *The New York Times* just reported 4 million subscribers, most of them digital, in its most recent quarterly earnings. That's the most in *NYT* history."[1]

Fake News

A major weapon in Trump's arsenal when jousting with the media was his use of the term "fake news."

According to *The Independent*, since December 2016, Trump used "fake news" more than 2,000 times, both online and in person.[2] In all his bombastic glory, he even claimed to have coined the phrase. Contrary to that, BuzzFeed editor Craig Silverman is credited with inventing the term in 2014. Trump may have appropriated the phrase, but he wielded it "as a cudgel to beat the media," Silverman said in his interview with *The Washingtonian*.[3]

If one reporter stands out as Trump's top adversary, it would have to be CNN correspondent Jim Acosta. Although many of Acosta's questions appear to have been legitimate in nature, he unfortunately allowed his disdain for Trump to consume him, resulting in prolonged bickering between the two. Oftentimes, this snatched precious time away from his colleagues.

A Nov. 7, 2018, news conference at the White House may have been the zenith of the feud between Trump and Acosta. During the event, Acosta refused to give a microphone back to a female White House staffer, and then stood and continued talking when Trump moved on to another reporter. As Trump engaged with the other reporter, Acosta stood up again, shouting at Trump.[4]

"When you report fake news, which CNN does a lot, you are the enemy of the people," Trump said.[5]

The same day, the White House suspended Acosta's media credentials, which prevented him from covering events at the presidential mansion. There was a brief legal tussle and Acosta's credentials were restored, but the White House established more stringent rules of engagement for future news conferences.[6]

"Nasty person"

Trump's feud with the mainstream media didn't end with his presidency, and in fact, resumed with equal fervor when he announced that he would seek a second term in challenging President Joe Biden in the 2024 election. One incident that exemplified this was the CNN hour-plus primetime town hall featuring Trump on May 10, 2023. Coincidentally, it was broadcast from my alma mater, St. Anselm College, in Manchester, New Hampshire, a longtime political venue in the Granite State.

Leading up to the town hall, CNN head Chris Licht stated in a January 2023 *LA Times* story that in the past, CNN may have appeared "too partisan, too quick to fall into political talking points," which likely dissuaded Republicans from appearing on the network.[7]

"The general sense was that you would not get a fair shake and you wouldn't be allowed to make your point," he told the *Times*. "I don't want CNN to be a place where you're going to have such a combative experience that you go fundraise off of it. It is best for our audience to understand where everybody is coming from."[8]

Rising star Kaitlan Collins was tapped to host the event, interviewing Trump and then opening the floor for questions from the crowd. Collins tried to be the tough-as-nails reporter, but, judging by the crowd reaction, ended up a human pincushion as Trump eviscerated her the majority of the time.

In one viral exchange, Collins asked Trump why he allegedly held onto documents that the federal government was supposedly seeking. Instead of then allowing Trump to answer, Collins continued to interrupt, prompting him to say, "You are a nasty person, I'll tell you," to the delight of many in the crowd.[9]

The only aspect I would have changed about the town hall would have been to tell Collins to pump the brakes on the over-the-top tough chick schtick. How about letting the man talk so that viewers can decide for themselves whether he is being genuine or not? If you let someone talk long enough, they either come out shining like a new dime or hanging themselves from the gallows.

Mugshot Breaks the Internet

The gaze was glowering, steely-eyed, vengeful, as if the man were looking right through the camera, locked on those who had leveled charges against him.[10]

It was historical in that there had never been a mugshot of a U.S. President, sitting or former, ever taken and released.[11]

Trump was, without a doubt, playing to his base as he posed for the mugshot that broke the internet after he voluntarily surrendered to authorities in Georgia on Aug. 24, 2023. The charges concerned Trump allegedly engaging in activity to alter the outcome of the 2020 election.[12] But if Trump's persecutors were hoping to break him, personally and publicly, the direct opposite occurred. The federal raid on Trump's Florida compound, Mar-a-Lago, following a series of indictments, proved to boost his popularity as the Republican frontrunner in the 2024 Presidential race, according to *Vanity Fair*.[13]

Trump's mugshot was the subject of numerous internet memes and his campaign seized on its popularity, printing the mugshot on T-shirts and posters.[14] Members of the black community, long thought to be firmly in the Democrat camp (remember Joe Biden's crack about "You ain't black if you vote for Trump"?[15]) began wearing mugshot t-shirts. This prompted former NBA great turned sports personality – and apparently bitter political pundit – Charles Barkley to say on CNN, "If I see a black person walking around with Trump's mugshot, I'm gonna punch 'em in the face."[16]

Here's something to consider: Many major media outlets now disavow using mugshots[17] when someone is accused of a crime, but when it came to Trump, there was a ravenous clamor for it. Trump had been indicted three other times, and each time, the media was salivating for a mugshot, and then lamenting and gnashing their teeth when one was not released to them. It appeared that there was not one outlet that had any misgivings – and I doubt hesitated for a millisecond – about publishing the mugshots of Trump and his accomplices in his fourth indictment. And from examining the mugshots, there are at least two minority co-defendants, Trevian Kutti and Harrison Floyd, who were also included. There has been no outcry over that either, as has been the case with mugshots of other minorities charged with crimes.[18] Could it be because these minorities are associated with Trump, who is seen as the devil incarnate by some in the media? How fair is that?

The whole mugshot fiasco seemed to backfire on the media because Trump didn't appear nervous, or pensive or scared. Not only did he take control of his appearance in his mugshot, he released it only 10 minutes after CNN – while boasting 20 million more followers on Twitter than the media outlet – and made millions in fundraising off merchandise. It was his first tweet since the platform reinstated him in November 2022.[19]

---

[1] Bloom, David. "Love It or Hate It, the Trump Show Has Been Very Good for Media Business." *Forbes*, November 5, 2018. https://www.forbes.com/sites/dbloom/2018/11/05/happy-election-season-media-donald-trump-has-been-very-good-for-you/?sh=62d9c01a3abd.

[2] Woodward, Alex. "'Fake News': A Guide to Trump's Favourite Phrase – and the Dangers It Obscures." *The Independent*, October 2, 2020. https://www.independent.co.uk/news/world/americas/us-election/trump-fake-news-counter-history-b732873.html.

[3] Beaujon, Andrew. "Trump Claims He Invented the Term 'Fake News' – Here's an Interview with the Guy Who Actually Helped Popularize It." *Washingtonian*, October 2, 2019. https://www.washingtonian.com/2019/10/02/trump-claims-he-invented-the-term-fake-news-an-interview-with-the-guy-who-actually-helped-popularize-it/.

[4] *Washington Post*. "Trump Calls CNN Reporter 'Rude, Terrible Person,' 'Enemy of the People.'" YouTube, November 7, 2018. https://www.youtube.com/watch?v=znndE1TR2UY.

[5] Ibid.

[6] Jansen, Bart, and William Cummings. "White House Backs Down from Fight with CNN, Restores Press Credential for Reporter Jim Acosta." *USA Today*, November 19, 2018. https://www.usatoday.com/story/news/politics/2018/11/19/jim-acosta-suspension-possibly-permanent/2053073002/.

[7] Battaglio, Stephen. "CNN Boss Chris Licht on Restoring Trust and Why He Deleted His Twitter Account." *Los Angeles Times*, January 30, 2023. https://www.latimes.com/entertainment-arts/business/story/2023-01-30/chris-licht-wants-cnn-to-be-news-on-cable-not-cable-news.

[8] Ibid.

[9] *The Telegraph*. "Donald Trump Cheered by Audience after Calling Presenter a 'Nasty Person' During CNN Town Hall." YouTube, May 11, 2023. https://www.youtube.com/watch?v=6B56wGAt1gc.

[10] "Mug Shot of Donald Trump." Wikipedia, August 24, 2023. https://en.wikipedia.org/wiki/Mug_shot_of_Donald_Trump.

[11] Frazier, Kierra. "What to Know About Trump's Mug Shot." Politico, August 24, 2023. https://www.politico.com/news/2023/08/24/trump-mug-shot-released-to-public-00112933.

[12] Alexander, Blayne, et al. "Trump and 18 Co-Defendants Charged with Racketeering in Georgia 2020 Election Probe." NBC News, August 14, 2023. https://www.nbcnews.com/politics/donald-trump/trump-indicted-georgia-racketeering-rcna74912.

[13] McCordick, Jack. "Trump's Support Among Republicans Increased After Criminal Indictments: Poll." *Vanity Fair*, June 25, 2023. https://www.vanityfair.com/news/2023/06/trump-poll-increases-after-indictments.

[14] Woodward, Alex. "Trump Has Raised Millions with His Mug Shot. Legal Experts Say It Could Be a Big Mistake." Yahoo! News, September 4, 2023. https://news.yahoo.com/trump-raised-millions-mug-shot-195728637.html?fr=sycsrp_catchall.

[15] @HipHollywood. "Joe Biden to Charlamagne: 'You Ain't Black' If You Vote for Trump!" YouTube, May 22, 2020. https://www.youtube.com/watch?v=We6Qr9-dDn8.

[16] CNN. "Gayle King: I Was Insulted by Trump's Comments About Black Voters." YouTube, March 5, 2024. https://www.youtube.com/watch?v=djCKmQVkftY.

[17] Poynter, "Newsrooms are rethinking their use of mugshots in crime reporting." Feb. 11, 2020. https://www.poynter.org/ethics-trust/2020/newsrooms-are-rethinking-their-use-of-mugshots-in-crime-reporting/.

[18] Wang, Claire. "Why some local news outlets won't post mugshots – and are reimagining the crime beat." NBCUAcademy, June 15, 2021. https://nbcuacademy.com/claire-wang-mugshots-crime-beat-police/.

[19] O'Kane, Caitlin. "In His First Tweet in More than Two Years, Trump Shares His Mug Shot on X." CBS News, August 25, 2023. https://www.cbsnews.com/news/donald-trump-mug-shot-tweet-twitter-x-return/.

Chapter 8 – Elon Musk

Multi-billionaire Elon Musk has, what John Goodman's loan shark character Frank, calls "f**k you money" in the 2014 movie *The Gambler*. It refers to having accumulated enough wealth that you can do, essentially, whatever you want. If someone asks you to do something you don't want to do, the answer is "F**k you."[1]

Having that kind of money might also manifest in other ways, like, oh I don't know, enabling you to launch your own flamethrower company, which Musk did in 2018, selling some 20,000 of the novelties for the coming zombie apocalypse.[2] But possessing your own social media platform to espouse your newly-declared "free speech absolutist" views might be seen as the pinnacle of "f**k you money." Musk did it on October 27, 2022, when he purchased Twitter for $44 billion.[3] Around that time, he stated on Twitter, "Free speech is essential to a functioning democracy."[4]

Not long after seizing control, Musk terminated CEO Parag Agrawal, CFO Ned Segal, and legal affairs and Policy Chief Vijaya Gadde.[5] Around that time, revelations about the platform's deep connections to several U.S. federal government agencies – and its subsequent acquiescence to their requests to censor certain accounts – began to percolate.[6]

"Under former Twitter employees' watch, Twitter devolved into a private company the FBI and federal government infiltrated to deliberately limit free speech, particularly conservative speech and news contrary to the mainstream narrative," according to a news release published Feb 8, 2023, by the U.S. House of Representatives Committee on Oversight and Accountability.[7]

Less than a year after the acquisition, many in the mainstream media expressed displeasure with Musk's new policies, as *The Atlantic*'s Adam Serwer branded him a "right wing billionaire" (funny that, since Musk says he voted for Biden in 2020) in a story titled "Elon Musk's Free-Speech Charade Is Over."[8]

"The mogul's treatment of union organizers and whistleblowers suggested that 'free-speech absolutism' was mostly code for a high tolerance for bigotry toward particular groups, a smoke screen that obscured an obvious hostility toward any speech that threatened his ability to make money," Serwer wrote.[9]

Musk's acquisition of Twitter – which he later renamed X – signaled the demise of the platform's censorship reign of terror, highlighted by the dissolution of its relationship with federal agencies. To the mainstream media, this was a glitch in the matrix – they couldn't handle it – and so they responded with a sneering jealousy over his billions and an aggressive dubiety toward his free speech values.

Wielding the Ban-Hammer

Musk again drew the ire of the mainstream media when he temporarily banned the accounts of several prominent reporters, including those from *The New York Times*, *Washington Post,* and CNN in December 2022. The journalists reported on a dispute between Musk and a Twitter user, ElonJet, who posted the real-time locations of Musk's private jet.[10]

Musk said he viewed the culprit's actions and, subsequently, the journalists' parroting of the information, as potentially placing his family in danger.

"They posted my exact real-time location, basically assassination coordinates, in (obvious) direct violation of Twitter terms of service ... Same doxxing rules apply to 'journalists' as to everyone else," Musk tweeted.[11]

The term "doxxing" is most likely derived from "dropping the documents" on someone, meaning the intentional, oftentimes malicious release of sensitive information to the internet, including home address, phone numbers, and family members. Doxxing can result in exposing the target to online harassment and other crimes, either online or in-person, according to CNN.[12]

Roger McNamee, managing director of the private equity firm Elevation Partners, told MSNBC that Musk's actions amounted to "a direct attack on journalism and, by extension, on democracy. And I think policymakers and journalists have to go to battle stations here."[13]

Interesting how there was nary a public outcry from politicians and journalists when the accounts of conservative voices like Donald Trump, Marjorie Taylor Greene, the Babylon Bee, Jordan Peterson, Andrew Tate, and Project Veritas were banned on Twitter. Conversely, some in the mainstream media appeared to take an inordinate amount of glee in the suspensions, particularly Trump's.[14] Accounts of journalists in the ElonJet incident were restored by Musk about a day later, in the name of free speech and the phrase, "*vox populi, vox dei,*" Latin for "The voice of the people is the voice of God."[15]

Another skirmish between Musk and the media took place in April 2023 when he began attaching labels, including "state-funded media" and later "government-funded media," to the accounts of such outlets as PBS, NPR, BBC, and CBC. When NPR complained about the label, Musk tweeted, "NPR literally says Federal funding is *essential* on their website right now at ...What have you got against the truth @NPR?"[16]

The link Musk posted leads to a portion of NPR's website titled "Public Radio Finances," which reads, "Federal funding is essential to public radio's service to the American public and its continuation is critical for both stations and program producers, including NPR."[17]

NPR's Mary Yang disagreed with the Twitter labels, writing, "That label was misleading: NPR receives less than 1% of its $300 million annual budget from the federally funded Corporation for Public Broadcasting and does not publish news at the government's direction."[18]

Later the same month, Musk removed all of the labels, but most of the outlets did not resume tweeting. On April 12, 2023, NPR announced it was "stepping away from Twitter." They did not return, although two months to the day later, their brand was associated with Twitter in an article on The Post Millennial's website titled "NPR traffic PLUMMETS after rage quitting Twitter."[19]

"According to web analytics firm Similarweb, npr.org went from 111.5 million page visits in March to 104.2 million in May, a decrease of over seven million," according to the story, written by Jarryd Jaeger. "During that time, the website dropped four spots in the United States, landing at 143rd most popular."[20]

CNBC Taken Behind the Woodshed

In the spring of 2023, Musk sat for two high-profile interviews which saw him verbally grapple with his interviewers. In one, CNBC's David Faber asked Musk why he engaged in conspiracy theories online.

"Yes, but honestly, some of these conspiracy theories have turned out to be true," Musk said.

"Which ones?" Faber asked.

"Well like the Hunter Biden laptop."

"That's true."

"That was a pretty big deal, there was ... Twitter and others engaged in active suppression of information that was relevant to the public," Musk said. "That's a terrible thing that happened. That's election interference."[21]

Battling the BBC

In April 2023, Musk was interviewed by BBC reporter James Clayton. During the interview, Musk rejected the "niche" of San Francisco-Berkeley politics that had ruled Twitter before his purchase and said it needed to be a digital town square for the world.[22]

"In order for something to serve as a digital town square, it must serve people from all political persuasions, provided it's legal," he said. "Free speech is meaningless unless you allow people you don't like to say things you don't like, otherwise it's irrelevant."[23]

Clayton's question about prioritizing freedom of speech over hate speech and misinformation triggered this exchange:

> "Who's to say that something is misinformation? Who's the arbiter of that? Is it the BBC?"
>
> —"You're literally asking me?"
>
> "Yeah."
>
> —"You are arbiter on Twitter because you own Twitter."
>
> "Yes, I'm saying who is to say that one person's misinformation is another person's information?"

Musk then says the point he is making is that the BBC has at times published things that are false. At Musk's questioning, Clayton said he felt certain the BBC had said things in the past that were not true.[24]

Squeezing the Lemon

Musk's contention with the media continued in 2024 with an unlikely source – former CNN journalist Don Lemon who, at the time of their interview, was contracted to launch a show on the X platform.

Lemon was fired from CNN on April 24, 2023. The *LA Times* appeared to imply that beneath the buttery-smooth voice and winsome smile lay a big ol' slice of hubris. "Lemon became the news, engaging in heated on-air clashes with his *CNN This Morning* co-hosts Poppy Harlow and Kaitlan Collins and sparking controversy with inflammatory statements about women's soccer and GOP presidential candidate Nikki Haley."[25]

The next month, after Lemon publicly expressed interest in starting his own show, Musk tweeted to him, "Have you considered doing your show on this platform? Maybe worth a try. Audience is much bigger."[26] With Musk's offer on the table, and possibly seeing the stratospheric success of Tucker Carlson's show on X, Lemon announced plans to launch a show on X called The Don Lemon Show in early 2024, with none other than Musk as his first guest.

But the show was doomed before it began. First, there were Lemon's alleged contract stipulations. You would expect cable broadcasters to have some ego to them, but how about possessing a head the size of the Hindenburg? According to *The New York Post*, Lemon demanded "a free Tesla Cybertruck, a $5 million upfront payment on top of an $8 million salary, an equity stake in the multibillion-dollar company, and the right to approve any changes in X policy as it relates to news content, according to a document reviewed by *The Post*."[27] And Radar reports another alleged contract rider was for an expense-free ride on a SpaceX rocket to host the "first podcast in space."[28] So if any of that was true, that's what Musk was probably mulling over going into the interview.

That aside, the interview itself was a verbal locking of horns, with each combatant attempting to exert their will over such issues as race, DEI (diversity, equity, and inclusion), and censorship. When the latter issue was discussed, Musk chided Lemon, "You want censorship so bad you can taste it."[29]

When Lemon broached the subject of the existence of racism in modern-day America, Musk responded, "If we keep talking about it non-stop, it will never go away. If we keep making it the central thing it will never go away."

"Why do you believe that?" Lemon asked.

"I think I'm just making a simple statement of fact ... So I think we want to get away from making everything a race or a gender or whatever issue and just treat people like individuals," Musk said.[30]

During the interview, Lemon also dedicated considerable time to X, suggesting that Musk has a responsibility to police the "hate speech" that finds its way onto the platform. Musk's response highlighted what he clearly considers one of the major shortcomings of mainstream media:

> "I think you'll find that when this is posted to the X platform, that people will reply to it with evidence ... If I say something that is inaccurate, I'm immediately corrected on the platform, that's the advantage of a real-time system like X. So there will be immediately in the replies, people correcting me, there will be a community note that will correct me, which is attached to the actual post itself."

"Do you think that as many people read that as reads your tweet?" Lemon queried.

"Yes ... If you consider the conventional media, that doesn't happen. Conventional media makes false statements all the time and nobody ever hears the correction," Musk said.31

Depending on who you talk to, Musk squeezed Lemon, or Lemon cornered Musk and made him squirm. Or maybe it was, as Star-Lord said, "a bit of both."32 It appeared that by the end of the hour-long exchange Lemon feared he may have torpedoed his relationship with the media mogul, as he said to Musk, "Honestly, I'm not trying to offend you," and then, within the same minute, "Again, I don't mean to upset you."33

Just hours after the interview, Musk shredded X's contract with Lemon.34

The Twitter Files

Musk, as owner of Twitter, sought to acknowledge the platform's past transgressions by allowing a small group of independent journalists unfettered access to Twitter's internal files and and to then disseminate their findings on the platform. Enter Matt Taibbi, formerly of *Rolling Stone*, Bari Weiss, a former *New York Times* opinion columnist, and Michael Shellenberger, a former public relations specialist-turned author, activist, and politician.35

According to Business Insider, Musk hand-picked the journalists because he recognized a common disruptor approach in their philosophy and work.

"Weiss and Taibbi are controversial figures who struck out alone after working for major media outlets. They share Musk's anti-establishment outlook, and have been granted the inside track on a major story," according to a BI story. "Weiss and Taibbi both abandoned high-profile roles to pursue their own reporting and are scathing critics of established outlets in their Substack newsletters."36

In the build-up to the 2020 election, pitting then-incumbent Donald Trump against challenger Joe Biden, Twitter colluded with Biden's team to censor any reference to *The New York Post*'s story on Hunter Biden's laptop, according to *The Spectator*'s Freddy Gray in a story, "How Twitter suppressed the Hunter Biden laptop story," on Dec. 3, 2022.[37]

The Post's story alleged that Joe Biden used his political influence as then-Vice President of the United States to coerce Ukrainian officials into sacking a prosecutor investigating Burisma, a company whose board on which Hunter Biden served.[38]

"The blockbuster correspondence – which flies in the face of Joe Biden's claim that he's 'never spoken to my son about his overseas business dealings' – is contained in a massive trove of data recovered from a laptop computer," the story states.[39]

And just as the mainstream media either delayed or outright ignored the Hunter Biden laptop story – in order to ensure that Biden won the 2020 election[40] – they walked a similar path with the Twitter files reports about the laptop suppression.[41]

Between Trump and Musk, two of the most powerful, influential people in the world, a revolution of sorts was started. It was as if a wall had crumbled, and now to criticize, admonish, or otherwise disparage the previously-untouchable media was allowable. There was a revelation that the media was not a faceless machine, it was human, and humans are flawed; and sometimes those flaws need to be identified to foster its improvement.

---

[1] The Gambler (2014) - F*** You Scene (7/10) | Movieclips YouTube channel. https://www.youtube.com/watch?v=XamC7-Pt8No.

[2] 20,000 NOT-A-FLAMETHROWERS SOLD. https://www.boringcompany.com/not-a-flamethrower.

3 Stokel-Walker, Chris. "How Elon Musk Won Twitter." Wired, April 25, 2022. https://www.wired.com/story/elon-musk-buys-twitter-deal/.

4 Musk, Elon. "Free Speech Is Essential to a Functioning Democracy. Do You Believe Twitter Rigorously Adheres to This Principle?" Twitter, March 25, 2022. https://twitter.com/elonmusk/status/1507259709224632344?lang=en.

5 "Elon Musk Takes over Twitter, Parag Agrawal, Other Top Executives Fired." *The Economic Times*, October 28, 2022. https://economictimes.indiatimes.com/news/international/world-news/twitters-desi-ceo-parag-agrawal-legal-head-vijaya-gadde-on-way-out-as-elon-musk-confirms-acquisition/articleshow/95130369.cms?from=mdr.

6 "The Cover up: Big Tech, the Swamp, and Mainstream Media Coordinated to Censor Americans' Free Speech." United States House Committee on Oversight and Accountability, February 8, 2023. https://oversight.house.gov/release/the-cover-up-big-tech-the-swamp-and-mainstream-media-coordinated-to-censor-americans-free-speech-%EF%BF%BC/#:~:text=Under%20former%20Twitter%20employees'%20watch,contrary%20to%20the%20mainstream%20narrative.

7 Ibid.

8 Serwer, Adam. "Elon Musk's Free-Speech Charade Is Over." *The Atlantic*, April 12, 2023. https://www.theatlantic.com/ideas/archive/2023/04/elon-musk-twitter-free-speech-matt-taibbi-substack/673698/.

9 Ibid.

10 O'Brien, Matt. "Journalists Who Wrote About Owner Elon Musk Suspended from Twitter." PBS, December 16, 2022. https://www.pbs.org/newshour/nation/journalists-who-wrote-about-owner-elon-musk-suspended-from-twitter.

11 Musk, Elon. "Same Doxxing Rules Apply to 'Journalists' as to Everyone Else." Twitter, December 15, 2022. https://twitter.com/elonmusk/status/1603573725978275841.

12 Nguyen, Sen. "What is doxxing and what can you do if you are doxxed?" CNN.com, Feb. 7, 2023. https://www.cnn.com/2023/02/07/world/what-is-doxxing-explainer-as-equals-intl-cmd/index.html.

13 "McNamee: Musk Twitter Suspensions a 'Direct Attack' on Journalism & Democracy." Yahoo! News, December 16, 2022. https://news.yahoo.com/mcnamee-musk-twitter-suspensions-direct-041523019.html.

14 ABC News. "'Sway' podcast host Kara Swisher discusses Twitter, Facebook banning Trump." YouTube channel. https://www.youtube.com/watch?v=Q1aW4dCUACs.

15 Garg, Moohita Kaur, ed. "'Vox Populi, Vox Dei': Elon Musk Announces Reinstatement of Suspended Twitter Accounts." WION, November 25, 2022. https://www.wionews.com/world/twitter-has-spoken-millions-vote-yes-to-elon-musks-poll-on-reinstating-suspended-accounts-537242.

16 Musk, Elon. "NPR Literally Says Federal Funding Is *Essential* on Their Website Right Now…" Twitter, April 12, 2023. https://twitter.com/elonmusk/status/1646303780189900800.

17 "Public Radio Finances." NPR, accessed March 31, 2024. https://www.npr.org/about-npr/178660742/public-radio-finances.

18 Yang, Mary. "Twitter Removes All Labels About Government Ties from NPR and Other Outlets." NPR, April 21, 2023. https://www.npr.org/2023/04/21/1171236695/twitter-strips-state-affiliated-government-funded-labels-from-npr-rt-china.

19 Jaeger, Jarryd. "NPR Traffic Plummets After Rage Quitting Twitter." The Post Millennial, June 12, 2023. https://thepostmillennial.com/npr-traffic-plummets-after-rage-quitting-twitter.

20 Ibid.

21 Solovei, Dan. "Elon Musk Latest Interview with David Faber." YouTube, May 17, 2023. https://www.youtube.com/watch?v=Pf-smob2k50.

22 Burgess, Jean. "The 'Digital Town Square'? What Does It Mean When Billionaires Own the Online Spaces Where We Gather?" The Conversation, April 27, 2022. https://theconversation.com/the-digital-town-square-what-does-it-mean-when-billionaires-own-the-online-spaces-where-we-gather-182047.

23 Ibid.

24 Tesla Intelligence UK. "Full Elon Musk BBC Interview with Video and Timestamps 12th April 2023." YouTube, April 12, 2023. https://www.youtube.com/watch?v=IflfP4XwzAI&t=1232s.

25 Braxton, Greg. "Don Lemon Was the Brightest Star at CNN. Then He Became the Story." *Los Angeles Times*, April 25, 2023. https://www.latimes.com/entertainment-arts/tv/story/2023-04-25/don-lemon-cnn-fired-nikki-haley-vivek-ramaswamy-kaitlan-collins-poppy-harlow.

26 Musk, Elon. "Have You Considered Doing Your Show on This Platform? Maybe Worth a Try. Audience Is Much Bigger." Twitter, May 10, 2023. https://twitter.com/elonmusk/status/1656151522408026113?s=20.

27 Zilber, Ariel. "Don Lemon Demanded Tesla Cybertruck, $5m Advance, Equity in x Before Elon Musk Canned Him: Sources." *New York Post*, March 15, 2024. https://nypost.com/2024/03/15/media/don-lemon-demanded-tesla-cybertruck-5m-advance-equity-in-x-before-elon-musk-canned-him-sources/.

28 Surmonte, Connor. "Don Lemon Demanded Free Ride on Elon Musk's SpaceX Rocket to Host 'First Podcast in Space' Before X Ouster: Report." RadarOnline, March 20, 2024. https://radaronline.com/p/don-lemon-free-ride-elon-musk-spacex-rocket-first-podcast-space-report/.

29 Lemon, Don. "Elon Musk on Racism, Bailing Out Trump, Hate Speech, and More – the Don Lemon Show (Full Interview)." YouTube, March 18, 2024. https://www.youtube.com/watch?v=hhsfjBpKiTw.

30 Ibid.

31 Lemon, Don. "Elon Musk on Racism, Bailing Out Trump, Hate Speech, and More – the Don Lemon Show (Full Interview)." YouTube, March 18, 2024. https://www.youtube.com/watch?v=hhsfjBpKiTw.

32 @jnl425. "Guardians of the Galaxy - Ending Scene (Ain't No Mountain High Enough)." YouTube, June 3, 2017. https://www.youtube.com/watch?v=XuYmQ-WRMFE.

33 Lemon, Don. "Elon Musk on Racism, Bailing Out Trump, Hate Speech, and More – the Don Lemon Show (Full Interview)." YouTube, March 18, 2024. https://www.youtube.com/watch?v=hhsfjBpKiTw.

34 Harris, Raquel "Rocky." "Don Lemon Questions Why Elon Musk Fired Him but Is 'Not Complaining' About Tucker Carlson | Video." Yahoo!, March 20, 2024. https://www.yahoo.com/entertainment/don-lemon-questions-why-elon-010046697.html?fr=sycsrp_catchall.

35 *The Western Journal*, Dec. 9, 2022. https://www.westernjournal.com/can-read-twitter-files-right/.

36 Dodgson, Lindsay. "Musk's media renegades: The anti-establishment writers including Matt Taibbi and Bari Weiss chosen for the 'Twitter Files.'" Business Insider, Dec. 12. 2022. https://www.businessinsider.com/journalists-helping-elon-musk-twitter-files-2022-12.

37 Gray, Freddy. "How Twitter suppressed the Hunter Biden laptop story." *The Spectator*, Dec. 3, 2022. https://www.spectator.co.uk/article/how-twitter-suppressed-the-hunter-biden-laptop-story/.

38 Morris, Emma Jo, and Gabrielle Fonrouge. "Smoking-gun email reveals how Hunter Biden introduced Ukrainian businessman to VP dad." *The New York Post*, Oct. 14, 2020. https://nypost.com/2020/10/14/email-reveals-how-hunter-biden-introduced-ukrainian-biz-man-to-dad/.

39 Ibid.

[40] Flood, Brian. "Liberal media 'snuffed out' Hunter Biden coverage until after election to help defeat Trump, critics say." Fox News, Dec. 10, 2020. https://www.foxnews.com/media/liberal-media-ignored-hunter-biden-scandal-election-defeat-trump.

[41] Kpoenig, Melissa. "What are you hiding? Liberal media fails to cover Hunter Biden 'smoking gun' Twitter emails AGAIN... amid questions over whether they were also told by FBI to ignore the first son's laptop." DailyMail.com, Dec. 20, 2022. https://www.dailymail.co.uk/news/article-11558785/MSM-fail-cover-Hunter-Biden-smoking-gun-Twitter-emails-AGAIN.html.

Chapter 9 – Media Sows Distrust and Pays the Price

Over the past several years, Americans found themselves at a crossroads – either continue to pay for news services they viewed as divisive and untrustworthy, or give them the proverbial heave-ho and go elsewhere; you might say their theme song was Twisted Sister's "We're Not Gonna Take It."

Thinking on this, I developed a hypothesis. The reason mainstream media has experienced plummeting audiences, readership and ratings was, quite simply, due to America's growing dissatisfaction with how the news was presented. After all, if you are a consumer, why would you want to invest your money and attention in a product that you believe is attempting to purposely mislead or patronize you?

Newspapers, the oldest form of media in America, withstood the onslaught of radio and television, even cable, but more than likely the emergence of the internet and newspapers' subsequent reluctance to hop onboard proved to be an insurmountable hurdle. In 2000, the total estimated weekday circulation of U.S. daily newspapers was 55.8 million. That dropped to 24.2 million by 2020, according to Editor & Publisher and the Pew Research Center, reported by census.gov.[1] That's more than half in two decades!

The slow decline for both cable and broadcast news appeared to start in 2010, according to a story from The Hollywood Reporter: "After years of audience growth, cable news may have hit a wall. According to the Project for Excellence in Journalism's annual State of the News Media report, cable news viewership for CNN, MSNBC and Fox News fell substantially in 2010 — 13.7 percent in aggregate for a sharper decline than any other sector. Broadcast news, which has experienced declining viewership for years, was down another 3.4 percent in 2010."[2]

Jumping ahead more than a decade, ratings woes continued for the godfather of cable news, CNN: "February marked CNN's lowest-rated month in a decade, with the network's prime time lineup dropping 42% among viewers 25-54—the key demographic group valued by advertisers—compared to the same month one year ago," according to a Forbes.com story.[3]

A 2023 article from pewresearch.org gives a snapshot of the news industry:

- Daily newspaper circulation continued to nosedive. The top three newspapers in the country experienced digital growth. That said, overall digital traffic to newspaper websites was down. Digital news websites also suffered a dip in traffic.

- Local TV news – morning, evening, and late-night slots – you guessed it, down. Cable news received an audience bump during the pandemic, but then slipped in 2021. Fox News surged again in 2022. Network news on the big three – ABC, CBS and NBC – remained stable.

- Terrestrial radio found itself in a nosedive, but there is an escalation in podcast and online audio listening.[4]

We've established that things have not gone as planned for the mainstream media in terms of how many eyeballs it would like on its products. Now let's talk about dissatisfaction among audiences. Several studies in the 2020s appear to indicate a marked mistrust and malcontent with the mainstream media. A Feb. 15, 2023 story from the Associated Press reveals the results of a Gallup-Knight Foundation survey, indicating nearly half of Americans believe the media intends to misinform the public.5 One of the pollsters, Gallup's Sarah Feloni, described the results as "striking," adding that the findings "showed a depth of distrust and bad feeling that go beyond the foundations and processes of journalism."6

The story is indicative of the lack of introspection shared by journalists; they're so busy finding fault with everyone else, they can't or won't turn around and look at themselves in the mirror. I think if you were to ask members of the mainstream media, they would be incredulous that such results could be true, possibly suggesting that their audience is mistaken.

John Sands, Knight's senior director for media and democracy, noted that many of those who took the survey perceived a pattern of apathy or possibly ignorance by journalists. Americans don't seem to think that the national news organizations care about the overall impact of their reporting on the society."7

Another study produced a similar outcome. A May 23, 2023 story written by Bob Unruh discusses the results of a Rasmussen Reports survey conducted on May 16-18, 2023. In the survey, more than half – 52 percent – of likely voters said they have a profound distrust of the news. The same percentage stated they believe the media favors Democrats by more than 2 to 1. 6 And 59 percent agreed with the statement that the media are "truly the enemy of the people."8

The Associated Press, which reported on the Gallup-Knight Foundation study, conducted its own project in conjunction with the NORC Center for Public Affairs Research and the Robert F. Kennedy Human Rights. Released on May 1, 2023, the study indicated that "Nearly three-quarters of U.S. adults say the news media is increasing political polarization in this country, and just under half say they have little to no trust in the media's ability to report the news fairly and accurately."9

Speaking of polarization, that might be another cause of the decline in audience share among the mainstream media. There was a time when most news outlets appealed to individuals from all political persuasions. Now it appears that many are playing to their base, whether it be liberal or conservative, which effectively alienates them from a large group of people. Americans now gravitate to their own echo chamber to hear their beliefs repeated back to them, which in turn, makes them feel better about themselves.

CNN alluded to their polarizing coverage when they hired Chris Licht, according to the Anchorage Daily News.[10] "He's (Licht) told CNN's non-prime-time anchors they should leave opinions to the on-air guests," according to the story. "He has instructed staff to avoid presenting the extreme right and left of political issues, saying there "needs to be room for nuance ... 'We are truth-tellers, focused on informing, not alarming our viewers,' Licht wrote in a memo to employees."[11]

The story on the AP-NORC-RFK study also provided a clue as to one of the manifestations of the breakdown in trust between the media and the American public – an exodus to social media.[12] "That breakdown in trust may prompt many Americans to reject the mainstream news media, often in favor of social media and unreliable websites that spread misleading claims and that can become partisan echo chambers, leading to further polarization."[13]

From these surveys, we can see a dramatic decrease in the satisfaction the American public developed about the news, as if reporters and editors were tribes physically unconnected with the majority of the living, breathing world, but yet somehow still able to extend influence over it.

From all my searching, I couldn't find anything establishing that Americans' distrust and frustration with the media caused its ratings and readership to rupture. We can see that people are upset and also that the media is suffering, but not that one directly led to the other. Perhaps a study or survey can be initiated in an attempt to suss out this supposition.

I can tell you that anecdotally, as a reporter, I could feel the hostility online from people. I'm sure many of those folks had cancelled their subscription or were considering it.

---

[1] Grundy, Adam. "Service Annual Survey Shows Continuing Decline in Print Publishing Revenue." Census.gov, June 7, 2022. https://www.census.gov/library/stories/2022/06/internet-crushes-traditional-media.html#:~:text=There%20was%20a%20pronounced%20shift%20from%20print%20to,Editor%20%26%20Publisher%20and%20the%20Pew%20Research%20Center.

[2] Guthrie, Marisa. "Cable News Viewership Declines Double Digits in 2010." Hollywoodreporter.com, March 13, 2011. https://www.hollywoodreporter.com/tv/tv-news/cable-news-viewership-declines-double-167181/.

[3] Joyella, Mark. "CNN Hits 10-Year Low As Fox News Glides To Victory In Cable News Ratings." Forbes.com, Feb. 28, 2023. https://www.forbes.com/sites/markjoyella/2023/02/28/cnn-hits-10-year-low-in-prime-time-as-fox-news-glides-to-victory-in-february-cable-news-ratings/.

[4] Lipka, Michael and Shearer, Elisa. "Audiences are declining for traditional news media in the U.S. – with some exceptions." Pewresearch.org, Nov. 28, 2023. https://www.pewresearch.org/short-reads/2023/11/28/audiences-are-declining-for-traditional-news-media-in-the-us-with-some-exceptions/.

[5] Bauder, David. "Study Shows 'Striking' Number Who Believe News Misinforms." AP News, February 15, 2023. https://apnews.com/article/television-news-media-business-4367fdad2d6ce6c2c455195f9dfef908.

[6] Ibid.

[7] Ibid.

[8] Unruh, Bob. "Massive Number of Americans Say News Media ARE the Enemy." ClarkCountyToday.com, May 23, 2023. https://www.clarkcountytoday.com/news/massive-number-of-americans-say-news-media-are-the-enemy/.

[9] Klepper, David. "Americans Fault News Media for Dividing Nation: AP-NORC Poll." AP News, May 1, 2023. https://apnews.com/article/poll-

misinformation-polarization-coronavirus-media-d56a25fd8dfd9abe1389b56d7e82b873.

[10] Smith, Gerry. "New CNN Boss Seeks to Create a Less Divisive News Network." Anchorage Daily News, June 20, 2022. https://www.adn.com/nation-orld/2022/06/19/new-cnn-boss-seeks-to-create-a-less-divisive-news-network/.

[11] Ibid.

[12] Klepper, David. "Americans Fault News Media for Dividing Nation: AP-NORC Poll." AP News, May 1, 2023. https://apnews.com/article/poll-misinformation-polarization-coronavirus-media-d56a25fd8dfd9abe1389b56d7e82b873.

[13] Ibid.

Chapter 10 – Land of Layoffs

If a media entity produces content that is unacceptable to its readers or viewers, then it stands to reason they will withdraw their patronage; it's really basic supply-and-demand. With less money coming in, that equals less money to pay your staff. Therefore, one way to attempt to right the sinking ship is to jettison staff members. The conundrum created is that with fewer staff, a media entity produces even less original content, which likely frustrates customers, and so it becomes a vicious cycle.

In a June 2023 story on Axios, Sara Fischer wrote that so far that year, nearly 17,500 job cuts had been announced across the media, making it the highest job loss in the industry ever on record, according to a new report from Challenger, Gray & Christmas. And the year was only half over at that point.[1]

"The news industry is facing huge constraints due to a slowdown in the ad market, debt from consolidation and subscription fatigue," Fischer wrote.[2]

Subscription fatigue is defined by paddle.com as "a feeling of overwhelm and frustration experienced by consumers who find themselves inundated with subscription services and products."[3] My theory is that in everyone's head, there is a hierarchy of their subscriptions, from most needed to least. At the top you might have services like cable (for those still "plugged-in"), plus Amazon Prime, Netflix, Disney+ and so on. But where do news services fit in? I think for a lot of people, that's what gets the ax. Many of the 60 and over crowd still like the feeling of holding a physical newspaper in their hands. But generally anyone under that age will go online for their news. Yet online, there are plenty of sites that don't charge anything, so why go to a paid site? You'd have to be really dedicated to that entity in order to do so, or the website would have to provide a premium product that you just couldn't live without.

In one brutal example of bloodletting, *The Washington Post*, famous for its catchphrase "Democracy dies in darkness," decided to turn the lights out on the jobs of 240 employees in October 2023 by offering voluntary buyouts.

"In an email to staff, interim CEO Patty Stonesifer wrote that *The Post*'s subscription, traffic and advertising projections over the past two years had been 'overly optimistic' and that the company is looking for ways 'to return our business to a healthier place in the coming year.'"[4]

Nearly two months later, another email to staffers from Stonesifer surfaced on X, which read that 120 employees had accepted buyouts. No strangers to deadlines, she set Dec. 11 as the drop-dead day for non-union employees and Dec. 15 for union employees to get another 120 victims, er, volunteers.[5]

"We want everyone to understand that we need 240 acceptances to help restore *The Post*'s financial health," she said. "We have made the decision, if we fall short of this goal, to implement involuntary layoffs ... These layoffs would offer significantly less generous benefits than the voluntary package and will be consistent with prior layoff packages at *The Post*."[6]

So, basically give up your dream job and take one for the team or you might be forced to leave, and if we have to force you, you will get less money.

It's doubtful that the salaries and benefits of 240 staffers would even come close to off-setting the 2023 loss that *Post* rival *The New York Times* was predicting.

"*The Post* is on pace to lose about $100 million in 2023, according to two people with knowledge of the company's finances … *The Post* has struggled to increase the number of its paying customers since the 2020 election, when its digital subscriptions peaked at 3 million. It now has around 2.5 million."[7]

Breitbart writer John Nolte argued that the reason for such abysmal losses by *The Post* was that it consistently succumbed to reporting news stories – primarily pushed by leftists to smear conservatives – which later turned out to be hoaxes. Nolte counted 27 examples of such hoaxes, including the Jussie Smollett Hoax, the NASCAR Noose Hoax, and the Joe Biden Will Never Ban Gas Stoves Hoax.[8]

In April 2023, the generically-named "Paper" announced it was cutting all of its editorial staff. You might remember this was the joint that put a topless Kim Kardashian on its front cover in 2014, wearing what appeared to be a black trash bag below her highly-glazed and prodigious posterior. It was one of the first photos to "break the internet," so they claimed.[9]

"Publisher Tom Florio, who announced the layoffs, told staff that the advertising downturn of the last year prompted the decision. Paper follows in the footsteps of dozens of other digital media publishers, including Insider and BuzzFeed News, that have cut or shuttered titles in response to a depressed media buying climate," wrote Adweek's Mark Stenberg.[10]

As Stenberg's passage indicated, BuzzFeed News terminated 180 employees; also in 2023, Vox Media pink-slipped 130 workers, Insider cut 10 percent of its staff, ESPN said buh-bye to 300, and Vice Media filed for bankruptcy in a "restructuring," laying off 100 and deep-sixing its prestigious *Vice News Tonight* program.

Also in 2023, Warner Bros. Discovery laid off about 100 employees from its Discovery and Turner cable networks; Hearst Magazines sacked more than 40 positions from *Cosmopolitan, Elle,* and *Seventeen*; Spotify cut 800 jobs, *The Los Angeles Times* announced it would be cutting 74 positions in its newsroom, and MTV News was shuttered, according to forbes.com.[11]

The massacre continued in 2024, with more than 500 journalists laid off in January alone. *Sports Illustrated* fired nearly all of its staff, and Vice Media laid off hundreds and said they would cease publishing on vice.com – not sure where else they would publish content?[12]

And how exactly did The Messenger blow through $50 million in nine months? The website's concept showed promise proclaiming – non-partisan journalism – sadly, what was once an expectation in the industry was now something to be touted. Founder Jimmy Finkelstein and President Richard "Mad Dog" Beckman had some grandiose expectations, with Finkelstein saying he wanted the website "to recall great journalism institutions like *60 Minutes* and *Vanity Fair*."[13] Beckman predicted to *The New York Times* in April that the site would generate $100 million in revenue in 2024.[14]

The end came quickly, with some staffers seeing the writing on the wall and hightailing it, rather than waiting for the inevitable crash. A story from Mediaite contained a quote from an unnamed editor who skedaddled in May 2023. "I was told that this was going to be long-form journalism and all it was was aggregated content and clickbait, and to me, that's not journalism," she said.[15]

As I stated before, with fewer staff, there is more than likely going to be a decrease in the quality of the product or the amount of the product, or both, which could then lead to further losses of customers, so further down the toilet you go.

Over the span of two decades, I experienced newsrooms mutate from a boisterous, bustling incubator of ideas and laughter into a desolate, dystopian wasteland. It started with other departments in the office being farmed out overseas. Then there was consolidation on a national level; our dedicated, intelligent corps of copy editors was disbanded, replaced by a regional hub of faceless drones – I'm sure they were nice people, but we needed them in the newsroom, not in another state. When we were at full capacity, everyone had a beat, but then as reporters left, it was "We're not going to replace so-and-so, the investigative reporter. You'll just all have to add some investigative aspects to your work." Then there were straight-up layoffs. It reached the point where one publisher quit, citing that he did not want to be the ownership's hatchet-man.

This predicament was not constrained to York, Pennsylvania. According to the Neiman Lab, Gannett reduced its staff from 24,338 in 2018 to 11,200 in 2022. That's a drop of more than 50 percent in four years![16]

"Gannett's most recent annual report drives home the fact that no company has done more to shrink local journalism than it has in recent years ... Gannett has eliminated more than half of its jobs in the United States in four years. It's as if, instead of merging America's two largest newspaper chains (Gannett and

GateHouse in 2019), one of them was simply wiped off the face of the earth."[17]

The story goes on to draw a direct correlation between the gutting of newsrooms and a severe decrease in circulation for the chain: "There are plenty of explanations for the gap – but it's hard not to believe that Gannett's gutting of their editorial products hasn't been a driving factor."[18]

Gannett disputed the Neiman Lab story, stating in a news release that it misrepresented its circulation numbers and also its mission, stating, "We remain dedicated to serving communities by delivering trusted local journalism as we continue to focus on our opportunities for digital growth while evolving our legacy print business."[19]

The question remains, how long will this continue and what is the end game? Will newspapers and digital outlets continue to limp along, bleeding on borrowed time? As of this point, it doesn't seem that mainstream media has grown very introspective and thought, "Maybe we're the problem. Maybe we're dropping subscriptions faster than a buttered bullet because people don't trust us. Should we fundamentally change our news philosophy?" Some say this will never happen.

---

[1] Fischer, Sara. "Record Number of Media Job Cuts So Far in 2023." Axios, June 13, 2023. https://www.axios.com/2023/06/13/media-job-cuts-record.

[2] Ibid.

[3] Dormand, Chloe. "What Is Subscription Fatigue and How to Prevent It." Paddle, March 26, 2021. https://www.paddle.com/resources/subscription-fatigue.

[4] Tani, Max. "In a Memo to Staff, Washington Post CEO Patty Stonesifer Says 120 Employees Have Accepted Buyout Packages. If the Paper Doesn't Find Another 120 People Who Will Accept Buyouts in the Next Two

Weeks, It Will Implement Layoffs." Twitter, November 28, 2023. https://twitter.com/maxwelltani/status/1729540825561075981.

5 Ibid.

6 Ibid.

7 Mullin, Benjamin, and Katie Robertson. "A Decade Ago, Jeff Bezos Bought a Newspaper. Now He's Paying Attention to It Again." *The New York Times*, July 22, 2023. https://archive.is/SI1Vz#selection-493.0-497.158.

8 Nolte, John. "Nolte: Incredible Shrinking Washington Post Shrinks by 240 More Staffers." Breitbart, November 30, 2023. https://www.breitbart.com/the-media/2023/11/30/nolte-incredible-shrinking-washington-post-shrinks-by-240-more-staffers/.

9 Fortini, Amanda. "Break the Internet: Kim Kardashian." *PAPER Magazine*, November 12, 2014. https://www.papermag.com/break-the-internet-kim-kardashian-cover#rebelltitem1.

10 Stenberg, Mark. "Paper Magazine Lays Off Staff Due to Economic Headwinds." Adweek, April 26, 2023. https://www.adweek.com/media/paper-magazine-lays-off-staff/.

11 Washburn, Emily, and Ty Roush. "2023 Media Layoffs: CBC Cuts 10% of Workforce." *Forbes*, December 5, 2023. https://www.forbes.com/sites/emilywashburn/2023/12/05/2023-media-layoffs-cbc-cuts-10-of-workforce/?sh=1a3d6e114e40.

12 Roth, Emma. "Vice Is Abandoning Vice.Com and Laying Off Hundreds." The Verge, February 22, 2024. https://www.theverge.com/2024/2/22/24080497/vice-media-website-layoffs.

13 Steigrad, Alexandra. "Jimmy Finkelstein's Media Startup the Messenger Ripped over 'Delusional' Business Plan." *New York Post*, March 19, 2023. https://nypost.com/2023/03/19/critics-rip-jimmy-finkelstein-media-startup-the-messenger/.

14 Dugan, Kevin T. "How the Messenger Bled Out $50 Million." MSN, February 1, 2024. https://www.msn.com/en-us/money/companies/how-the-messenger-bled-out-50-million/ar-BB1hDm7a.

15 Luciano, Michael. "Massive Digital News Startup the Messenger Is Reportedly 'Out of Money' Already." Mediaite, October 23, 2023. https://www.mediaite.com/news/massive-digital-news-startup-the-messenger-is-reportedly-out-of-money-already/.

16 Benton, Joshua. "The Scale of Local News Destruction in Gannett's Markets Is Astonishing." NiemanLab, March 9, 2023. https://www.niemanlab.org/2023/03/the-scale-of-local-news-destruction-in-gannetts-markets-is-astonishing/.

[17] Ibid.

[18] Ibid.

[19] Schultz, Ray. "Gannett Disputes Nieman Lab Article on Circulation." Editor and Publisher, March 14, 2023. https://www.editorandpublisher.com/stories/gannett-disputes-niemanlab-article-on-circulation,242719.

Chapter 11 – Dreams Don't Pay the Bills

When conducting research for this book, I stumbled across an interesting find – journalism is the most-regretted major of college graduates, and by a fairly significant margin.

Searching around, I found several articles on the subject, dating back a few years. Sinem Buber, an economist at ZipRecruiter, wrote a story titled "The Most Regretted and Most Loved College Majors," published Nov. 3, 2022.[1] Journalism easily topped the list with 87 percent of graduates who said they would choose a different major if they had to do it all over again. In second-place is sociology with 72 percent.[2]

From an accompanying infographic, it appears ZipRecruiter commissioned the survey of 1,500 job seekers. They were asked one question – "If you could go back in time and select a college major all over again, knowing what you now know about the job market and the skills employers are looking for, what would you choose? Options: 1. I would choose the same major again, 2. I would choose a different major."[3]

Now if I were running the survey, I would have followed up with a second question – "Why do you regret majoring in ____?" Is it 1. Lack of fulfillment. 2. Low starting wage 3. Low earning potential 4. Subject to public ridicule 5. All of the above.

Buber's story does provide some clues: "Job seekers' feelings about their college majors are strongly tied to their job prospects later … Within each field, the most highly paid respondents are much more likely to be happy about their college major choice."[4]

It's only natural to want some return-on-investment after spending four years of your parents' money pulling all-nighters for midterms and finals, toiling over term papers, and guzzling coffee with your Spanish study group. Journalism has always been a big-on-fulfillment, short-on-compensation kind of job, but I think somewhere in the past decade or so a threshold was reached. Necessities like food, shelter, clothing, and the occasional beer or mixed drink were getting hard to afford.

But the caveat is that it's no secret you're not going to get rich as a journalist. According to payscale.com, the average annual base salary for a journalist is $45,423.[5] So if it's not the money they regret, what can it be?

Nearly a year after the survey was published, *The Federalist*'s Rebeka Zeljko revisited the original story and research, although venturing an educated guess as to why all the regret.[6]

"But modern J-school students, on the other hand, typically write massive tuition checks to be instructed in the propaganda that passes for journalism at most universities and in the insulated newsrooms their students populate," Zeljko wrote. "They are taught by people like *The New York Times*' Nikole Hannah-Jones, the author of the error-plagued revisionist history known as The 1619 Project, often at expensive 'elite' schools."[7]

Can it be concluded from this that journalism majors regret being indoctrinated in leftist ideology? Could we see a turning point in the industry on the horizon?

---

[1] Buber, Sinem. "The Most Regretted and Most Loved College Majors." ZipRecruiter, November 3, 2022.
https://www.ziprecruiter.com/blog/regret-free-college-majors/.

[2] Ibid.

[3] Ibid.

4 Ibid.

5 "Average Journalist Salary." Payscale, accessed March 31, 2024. https://www.payscale.com/research/US/Job=Journalist/Salary.

6 Zeljko, Rebeka. "Journalism Is 'Most Regretted' Major as Trust in Big Media Sinks." *The Federalist*, August 31, 2023. https://thefederalist.com/2023/08/31/study-shows-journalism-is-most-regretted-college-major-as-trust-in-corporate-media-sinks/#:~:text=A%20whopping%2087%20percent%20of,percent%20regret%20their%20chosen%20major.

7 Ibid.

Chapter 12 – Tucker Carlson Out at Fox News

Conservative powerhouse pundit Tucker Carlson's departure from Fox News, in April 2023, remains somewhat shrouded in mystery. Whatever the reason, it appears it superseded Carlson's standing as the company's franchise player. The powers-that-be most likely weighed out keeping him versus whatever viewership depletion they might experience from his abrupt ouster. Or maybe, for whatever reason, they felt they had no choice but to fire him? The world may never know.

It appeared, at least to Carlson, to be an unexpected development, as the host said to his audience on his last broadcast April 21, "Be back on Monday."

Following Tucker's expulsion, there was some swift shrinkage at Fox. According to *The Washington Post*, "In the four weeks before Carlson's exit, Fox averaged 2.6 million viewers in prime time; in the four weeks after, Fox averaged just 1.6 million – still at the top in cable news but down 39 percent."[1]

On June 20, 2023, Glenn Greenwald tweeted, "The 8pm slot on Fox with Tucker was not only consistently number 1 in the key demo - 25-54 - but routinely had 400,000 viewers or more. Without Tucker, it's crashed to worse-than-MSNBC levels: barely 100,000 people. Hannity is in 14th place, behind Joy Reid! A total collapse."[2]

There was gloating and rejoicing by adversaries of Carlson and Fox, but what they may not have realized is that Carlson leaving Fox crowned him the hottest free agent in all of the media industry, as he immediately began receiving offers from other conservative media outlets, as Glenn Beck's The Blaze[3], Russia Today (RT)[4] and MyPillow mogul Mike Lindell's LindellTV[5] all extended invitations to Carlson.

But, similar to other major personalities who left cable news – names like Beck, John Stossel, Megyn Kelly, and Bill O'Reilly – Carlson struck out on his own.

It would seem that with a non-compete clause in effect, Carlson as a news personality would be on the shelf until the 2024 Presidential election. But following his firing – and with Fox reportedly removing their studio equipment from Tucker's property in Maine[6] – Carlson and his crew quickly refurbished his studio.

In early May 2023, Carlson announced in a short video on Twitter that he would continue his show, now called "Tucker on Twitter." The first show hit the internet on June 6.

"I'm not working for Elon Musk ... what he's done is offered me what he's offered every other user of Twitter which is a chance to broadcast your views without a gatekeeper," Carlson later said in an interview with Russell Brand.[7]

Carlson's no-holds-barred, no-frills show, released weekly, featured the host sitting in his barn-studio, delivering news and opinion. With no corporate producer to rein him in, Carlson doubled-down as a steroid-infused gadfly of the left. His numbers on X have dwarfed anything on cable news, his interview with "Most Googled Person in the World" Andrew Tate garnered 110 million views, his sit-down with Russian President Vladimir Putin rose to 209 million, and his biggest to date, a skull session with former President Donald Trump, sits at 267 million views.[8]

Later in 2023, Carlson launched his own subscription streaming service, Tucker Carlson Network (TCN), featuring exclusive content on his website, tuckercarlson.com. Soon after, news of TCN's first advertising deal made headlines. "The agreement, worth at least $1 million, was reached with conservative-friendly shopping app Public Square... according to the app's CEO, Michael Seifert," wrote CNBC's Brian Schwartz.[9]

In the aforementioned interview with Russell Brand, Carlson talks about why he believed he was fired. Several weeks before his last broadcast, Carlson devoted a show to the January 6th tapes made available to him and his staff by then-Speaker of the House Kevin McCarthy. McCarthy allowed Carlson and his team access to the 40,000 hours of footage of the protest; however, he erred in not granting viewing permission to any other media outlet. If McCarthy was worried about the media not using what they saw for fear of it contradicting an "insurrection" narrative, there were other conservative outlets vying for the tapes.[10]

The March 6, 2023 episode of Tucker Carlson Tonight showed footage and commentary on what Carlson's team discovered, and was considered by some to be nothing short of a bombshell. Team Tucker was able to find two key pieces of evidence that certainly called into question some of the more popular narratives presented by the mainstream media as fact. In the episode, Carlson pointed out what appeared to be a coordinated effort to characterize the day as a "deadly insurrection."[11]

In an attempt to justify use of the word "deadly," Carlson posits that the media and politicians constructed a fictional account that Capitol Police Officer Brian Sicknick was murdered by the wrathful crowd.[12]

"The mob killed Officer Brian Sicknick, that's what they said," Carlson said. "It was their single-most powerful indictment of the January 6th protesters and of Donald Trump, and of Republican voters nationally."[13]

Many news outlets said Sicknick was struck in the head with a fire extinguisher during the protest.[14]

"It was a lie, untrue in any way," Carlson stated. "But only after that lie had hardened into conventional wisdom, did the newspaper (*The New York Times*) bother to retract it."[15]

Carlson then showed footage of Sicknick walking in the Capitol after he was supposedly "murdered" outside by the violent swarm of protesters. In the clip, Sicknick walks into view, his gait steady and balanced. He stops and directs a group of people inside the Capitol. Carlson states that his team found a marker on the tape indicating that investigators working for the Democrat-led January 6th Committee viewed the tape of Sicknick but buried it "because this tape would shatter the fraud they were perpetrating on the country."[16]

In connection with Sicknick waving a group of protesters inside the Capitol – as opposed to confronting them or otherwise barring their access – Carlson shows more footage of other protesters milling about the Capitol, with officers standing idly by or outright assisting their movements.[17]

"Taken as a whole, the video record does not support the claim that January 6th was an insurrection; in fact, it demolishes that claim," Carlson said.[18] This bombshell episode and the possibility of future episodes dedicated to additional footage may have caused concern among the bigwigs at Fox, or someone who had influence over them.

---

[1] Barr, Jeremy. "Fox News Regains Some Viewers Lost After the Firing of Tucker Carlson." *The Washington Post*, August 17, 2023. https://www.washingtonpost.com/media/2023/08/17/fox-news-ratings-rebound-jesse-watters-carlson/.

[2] Greenwald, Glenn. "The 8pm Slot on Fox with Tucker Was Not Only Consistently Number 1 in the Key Demo - 25-54 - but Routinely Had 400,000 Viewers or More. Without Tucker, It's Crashed to Worse-than-

MSNBC Levels..." Twitter, June 20, 2023.
https://twitter.com/ggreenwald/status/1671271081531908098.

3 Carbonaro, Giulia. "Tucker Carlson Offered Job by Ex-Fox Host After Leaving Network." *Newsweek*, April 25, 2023.
https://www.newsweek.com/tucker-carlson-job-ex-fox-news-host-1796469.

4 Woodward, Alex. "Russian State-Owned Media Offers Tucker Carlson a Job." *The Independent*, April 26, 2023.
https://www.independent.co.uk/news/world/americas/tucker-carlson-russian-state-tv-job-offer-b2327099.html.

5 McClure, Kelly. "'You're Welcome over Here': Mike Lindell Extends Job Offer to Tucker Carlson." Salon, April 29, 2023.
https://www.salon.com/2023/04/29/youre-welcome-over-here-mike-lindell-extends-job-offer-to-tucker-carlson/.

6 Hill, Michael P. "Fox Yanks Its Gear from Tucker Carlson's Maine Studio." NewscastStudio, May 25, 2023.
https://www.newscaststudio.com/2023/05/25/fox-tucker-carlson-studio-removed/#:~:text=Fox%E2%80%99s%20conservative%20commentary%20channel%20has%20removed%20the%20set,video%20panels%20a%20small%20full%20set%20and%20desk.

7 Brand, Russell. "'Stop Lying!!' | Tucker Carlson & Russell Brand Full Interview." YouTube, July 26, 2023.
https://www.youtube.com/watch?v=jjX3ntOmvQk.

8 Carlson, Tucker. Highlights by Tucker Carlson (@tuckercarlson) / ... Twitter, accessed March 31, 2024.
https://twitter.com/TuckerCarlson/highlights.

9 Schwartz, Brian. "Tucker Carlson Media Company Signs Its First Ad Deal." CNBC, November 8, 2023.
https://www.cnbc.com/2023/10/24/tucker-carlson-signs-first-ad-deal-since-fox-news-departure.html#:~:text=Former%20Fox%20News%20host%20Tucker%20Carlson's%20new%20media%20company%20has,the%20app's%20CEO%2C%20Michael%20Seifert.

10 Brand, Russell. "'Stop Lying!!' | Tucker Carlson & Russell Brand Full Interview." YouTube, July 26, 2023.
https://www.youtube.com/watch?v=jjX3ntOmvQk.

11 "Tucker Carlson Tonight (Full Episode) - Monday, March 6." Rumble, accessed March 31, 2024. https://rumble.com/v2c2tua-tucker-carlson-tonight-full-episode-monday-march-6.html.

12 Ibid.

13 Ibid.

[14] Ibid.
[15] Ibid.
[16] Ibid.
[17] Ibid.
[18] Ibid.

Chapter 13 – Reporters Fired for Social Media Vigilantism

In Chapter 4, I discussed the rise of reporter-activists and how damaging the movement has become to the craft of true journalism. As is the case with many radical ideologies, there appears to be, on at least some level, evidence of a correction.

The problem may be that reporters observe others on platforms like Twitter speaking their mind, and being invigorated by what they perceive is a lack of accountability at their respective media employers, decide that they too will assert themselves.

In February and March of 2023, two major media outlets – *The Dallas Morning News* and Axios – each fired one reporter for allegedly violating their respective professional journalism policies.

Axios terminated reporter Ben Montgomery after he responded in snarky fashion to a news release from Florida Gov. Ron DeSantis,[1] while Meghan Mangrum was fired from the *Dallas Morning News* after she took to Twitter and chastised Dallas Mayor Eric Johnson, addressing him by using the term "bruh."[2]

Were the firings symbolic of an industry-wide backlash to reporters overstepping their bounds, a sort of accountability enforcement, or were media companies simply looking for any excuse to save money by trimming remaining chaff from the staff? It's hard to say.

In Montgomery's case, according to *The New York Post*, DeSantis' office pushed out a press release focusing on the governor hosting a roundtable titled, "Exposing the Diversity Equity and Inclusion (DEI) Scam in Higher Education." But Montgomery emailed this response: "This is propaganda, not a press release."[3]

But press releases essentially *are* propaganda – "the spreading of ideas, information, or rumor for the purpose of helping or injuring an institution, a cause, or a person."[4] Honestly, what did Montgomery expect? DeSantis' office certainly wasn't going to disseminate anything that would reflect negatively on them; they were playing to their conservative base, many of whom have serious misgivings about DEI.

"Montgomery told *The Washington Post* he received a call from Jamie Stockwell, the executive editor of Axios Local, on Monday evening with his boss asking if he sent the email," according to *The New York Post*. "She then told the reporter his 'reputation in the Tampa Bay area' had been 'irreparably tarnished,' Montgomery said."[5]

At this point in the chapter, I feel like I'm in the movie *Groundhog Day*, living the same day over and over again with yet another reporter swerving out of their lane, spouting their unsolicited opinion like an old man yelling at the clouds.

The incident involving Mangrum began in February 2023, when Dallas Mayor Eric Johnson tweeted about the city's decline in violent crime and also noted the hypocrisy that had the news been negative, the media would have assuredly covered it.

"Our local media have no interest in reporting on this data, which is why you haven't heard about it. But you better believe if Dallas was leading the nation in violent crime INCREASES you'd be hearing about it daily. It's sad, really. Kudos to @DallasPD and our residents!" Johnson tweeted. "And as we've seen recently, if policing or crime stories don't feed into a particular narrative, the national media has zero interest in them. If it doesn't feed into our worst tribal instincts or show a city devolving into violent crime-ridden chaos, the media will not cover it."[6]

Mangrum, an education reporter, responded with a tweet: "Bruh, national news is always going to chase the trend. Cultivate relationships with quality local news partnerships."[7]

Johnson fired back. "Bruh? Have we met?"[8] and then later added: "Gotta love when folks let their inherent biases show. I get to be addressed as 'bruh' by someone who writes for my daily local paper whom I've never met."[9]

First, Mangrum says "bruh." That's a slang term, similar to "bro," but when the user is in a state of incredulousness, like when you're having a conversation with your friend and he says something ridiculous. You begin your response with "Bruh ..." It's not typically used in a professional setting, let alone for a public official. It shows a lack of respect for the official, the office, or those who elected him, many of whom are readers. To be fair, Johnson did call reporters "hit dogs" on Twitter[10] after the exchange with Mangrum, which he later clarified by writing, "Oh, and my grandmother used to say 'If you throw a rock at a pack of dogs, the one that hollers is the one that got hit.'"[11]

Second, Mangrum says "national news is always going to chase the trend." What trend? Violence in cities? I'd say that is something the *Dallas Morning News* should be covering. Leave national news to the wire services. I'd be willing to bet the people buying the *Dallas Morning News* care more about what's going on in Dallas.

Finally, her imperative to "cultivate relationships with quality local news partnerships"[12] smacks of a holier-than-thou attitude. Who's to say Johnson is not doing just that? His office probably doesn't communicate on a regular basis with an education reporter. I'm sure the paper has both political and crime reporters that have relationships with his office.

Mangrum was quoted in a *D Magazine* interview as saying she felt her colleagues were under fire and so she needed to defend them.[13] It makes one wonder if the vehicle of social media is a factor here. Long before the internet, most media outlets had a code of conduct for journalists, which may have varied, but typically included some of the following:

- Don't accept gifts from sources or anyone else when you are on-the-job.
- Don't get arrested (unless it's in support of the First Amendment).
- Pursue the truth relentlessly and be objective in your reporting.
- Don't do anything that would embarrass you, the craft of journalism, or the newspaper.

Of course, it was understood that you keep your opinions to yourself.

Taking Sides in an Eons-old Conflict

On Saturday, Oct. 7, 2023, Hamas terrorists staged a coordinated, clandestine attack on the Israeli nation, killing innocents with impunity.[14]

Not surprisingly, those who believe others actually care what they think – including actors, athletes, and college students – took to social media, many supporting Hamas' atrocities. And wouldn't you know, there was a reporter who hopped on X to spout off. As I have said many times before, as a reporter, if you want to establish and maintain credibility, keep it professional, leave emotion out of the equation. If you want to rant about a political, global, or societal conflagration, get your colleagues together for a beer at the local watering hole.

Apparently, Jackson Frank, a reporter who covered the Philadelphia 76ers for PhillyVoice.com, didn't get the memo. The Sixers tweeted this after word spread of the attacks: "We stand with the people of Israel and join them in mourning the hundreds of innocent lives lost to terrorism at the hands of Hamas. #StandWithIsrael." The mustache and mullet-wearing Frank replied with, "This post sucks! Solidarity with Palestine always."[15]

Punishment came quickly to Frank, as *The New York Post* tracked down PhillyVoice.com CEO Hal Donnelly, who said, "Mr. Frank is no longer employed by PhillyVoice.com as of today. We stand with everyone who is absolutely outraged by the senseless attacks in Israel, by the loss of innocent lives and violence against civilians."[16]

In addition to sharing my view that reporters should not express their opinions on social media, website Larry Brown Sports brings up another solid point about professionalism and credibility in journalism: "A critical tenet of journalism is to treat your subjects fairly and not show bias. Frank's social media post very clearly demonstrated a negative bias against the team he was hired to cover."[17]

Exactly. Say Frank was not fired. He would have been branded in perpetuity as the guy who covers the Sixers but lambasted them for their support of Israel. He would never be able to shake the suspicion of having a bias against the team.

---

[1] Propper, David. "Axios Reporter Fired After Accusing Desantis Press Shop of Pushing 'Propaganda.'" *New York Post*, March 15, 2023. https://nypost.com/2023/03/15/journalist-ben-montgomery-fired-from-axios-after-email-to-desantis-office/.

2 Serrano, Jody. "Dallas Reporter: I Was Fired for Calling the Mayor 'Bruh' on Twitter." Gizmodo, March 2, 2023. https://gizmodo.com/dallas-morning-news-bruh-mayor-tweet-meghan-mangrum-1850179389#:~:text=A%20reporter%20says%20she%20was%20fired%20by%20her,up%20to%20Mayor%20Eric%20Johnson%2C%20D%20Magazine%20reported.

3 Propper, David. "Axios Reporter Fired After Accusing Desantis Press Shop of Pushing 'Propaganda.'" *New York Post*, March 15, 2023. https://nypost.com/2023/03/15/journalist-ben-montgomery-fired-from-axios-after-email-to-desantis-office/.

4 Shpanser, Noam. "The Con of Propaganda." *Psychology Today*, February 15, 2017. https://www.psychologytoday.com/us/blog/insight-therapy/201702/the-con-propaganda.

5 Propper, David. "Axios Reporter Fired After Accusing Desantis Press Shop of Pushing 'Propaganda.'" *New York Post*, March 15, 2023. https://nypost.com/2023/03/15/journalist-ben-montgomery-fired-from-axios-after-email-to-desantis-office/.

6 Johnson, Mayor Eric L. "Them Hit Dogs Still Hollerin'! And Still Clearly Unable or Unwilling to Read Carefully a Simple Tweet. Explains Why the Media Is Where It Is in Terms of Public Opinion: The Quality Has Fallen off a Cliff. Pathetic." Twitter, February 11, 2023. https://twitter.com/Johnson4Dallas/status/1624487311370080258?ref_src=twsrc%5Etfw%7Ctwcamp%5Etweetembed%7Ctwterm%5E1624487311370080258%7Ctwgr%5E741a8fc0cb6c012b252ec0804d4c2dd8da27b3d0%7Ctwcon%5Es1_&ref_url=https%3A%2F%2F167.172.241.183%2Fpublications%2Fd-magazine%2F2023%2Fapril%2Fis-dallas-really-the-safest-big-city-in-america%2F.

7 Keane, Isabel. "Dallas Journalist Meghan Mangrum Claims She Was Fired for Calling Mayor 'Bruh' on Twitter." *New York Post*, March 2, 2023. https://nypost.com/2023/03/02/dallas-journalist-fired-for-calling-mayor-bruh-on-twitter/.

8 Serrano, Jody. "Dallas Morning News Reporter Says She Was Fired for Calling the Mayor 'Bruh' on Twitter." Yahoo! News, March 2, 2023. https://news.yahoo.com/dallas-morning-news-reporter-says-185528664.html?fr=sycsrp_catchall.

9 Johnson, Mayor Eric L. "Gotta Love When Folks Let Their Inherent Biases Show. I Get to Be Addressed as 'Bruh' by Someone Who Writes for My Daily Local Paper Whom I've Never Met." Twitter, February 11, 2023. https://twitter.com/Johnson4Dallas/status/1624491098591621130.

10 Goodman, Matt. "Is Dallas Really the Safest Big City in America?" *D Magazine*, April 13, 2023. https://www.dmagazine.com/publications/d-magazine/2023/april/is-dallas-really-the-safest-big-city-in-america/.

11 Ibid.

12 Keys, Matthew. "Fired Dallas Reporter Complains About Media Coverage." The Desk, March 7, 2023. https://thedesk.net/news/meghan-mangrum-ungrateful-dallas-reporter-fired-tweet-union-contract/.

13 Rogers, Tim. "Dallas Morning News Fires Reporter for Calling Mayor 'Bruh' on Twitter." *D Magazine*, March 1, 2023. https://www.dmagazine.com/frontburner/2023/03/dallas-morning-news-fires-reporter-for-calling-mayor-bruh-on-twitter/.

14 "Israel/Palestine: Videos of Hamas-Led Attacks Verified." Human Rights Watch, October 18, 2023. https://www.hrw.org/news/2023/10/18/israel/palestine-videos-hamas-led-attacks-verified.

15 Estudillo, Itiel. "NBA Journalist Covering 76ers Fired After Criticizing Team's Israel Tweet." MSN, October 10, 2023. https://www.msn.com/en-us/sports/nba/nba-journalist-covering-76ers-fired-after-criticizing-teams-israel-tweet/ar-AA1hXqgt.

16 Glasspiegel, Ryan. "76ers Beat Writer Out at PhillyVoice after Ripping Team's Israel Tweet." *New York Post*, October 9, 2023. https://nypost.com/2023/10/09/76ers-beat-writer-out-at-phillyvoice-after-ripping-teams-israel-tweet/.

17 Brown, Larry. "Reporter Fired for Social Media Post Ripping 76ers over Israel Support." Larry Brown Sports, October 9, 2023. https://larrybrownsports.com/basketball/reporter-jackson-frank-fired-76ers-israel-support/621959.

Chapter 14 – The Dawn of Independent/Citizen Journalists

The traditional journalist, more than likely employed by a newspaper chain, website, or TV network, may be going the way of the Tasmanian Tiger. Trained at a college or university, some critics believe they are indoctrinated with "woke" ideology and become loyal foot soldiers who are then deployed into the world, masquerading as paragons of truth. Others dismiss this as conspiracy theory, saying today's journalists are pure of heart and are ensuring that "democracy" – which now appears to be a weaponized word – is preserved in the U.S.

History has shown us that when one civilization, business, or cultural trend falls, another rises up to take its place, and not only that, but often it engineers the downfall of its predecessor. So it may be with mainstream media and independent and citizen journalism. The leviathan that is mainstream media has become so vast and its operators so reckless and vainglorious, it is now a soft target. That's where independent journalism has stepped in.

In Chapter 9, I chronicled the paradigm shift in news consumption, as many citizens across America have said that what passes for news is merely thinly-veiled propaganda. And so they have voted with their money and attention. Just take a look at the papers whose newsrooms have been gutted; take a look at CNN's hemorrhaging viewership, according to an AP story published March 30, 2023, by David Bauder.[1]

But, as I have often said, "The news doesn't report itself." Well, not yet (we see you, AI). It stands to reason that if viewers and readers are not getting their news from mainstream media, they're getting it somewhere else.

Concurrent with the public's move away from traditional news, we have seen the advent of the smartphone – in particular, the advancements in its camera technology – and the dawn of massive social media platforms like Twitter (X) and Facebook with exponential reach. So now we have the motive, the means, and the capability... and shazam! Everyone who owns a smartphone has the potential to be a citizen journalist, and many owners, at one time or another, probably have been.

Some of the most popular videos on the internet are those that have been shot at real events by regular folks. Now if only we could teach them how to hold the camera steady, use features like focus and zoom, and for God's sake, turn it lengthwise for a more cinematic effect, but hey, baby steps, right?

Another pivotal factor is that the internet is the ultimate equalizer. If you have a camera, some moxie, and a platform, you can be an independent media source. Then, if you get a major platform that actually supports what you're doing, even better. Enter, once again, Elon Musk. In a 2022 article on Axios, Musk pledged his willingness to harness the power of X to elevate independent/citizen journalism.

"When asked about the role that the traditional press should play on Twitter, Musk has said that he believes in 'citizen journalism' as a way to counter the mainstream media's power," Sara Fischer of Axios wrote. "I'm not saying we should somehow downplay the major publications or prominent journalists. I'm simply saying we should elevate people and give voice to the people. Much more."[2]

You want to talk about the power of social media? Take a look at this headline: "TikTok and Instagram influencers top list of trusted news sources for today's youth."[3]

According to a Fox News story written by Lawrence Richard, "A study conducted for the Reuters Institute for the Study of Journalism, part of Britain's University of Oxford, found 55% of TikTok users and 52% of Instagram users get their news from 'personalities' on the respective platforms."[4]

Nic Newman, senior research associate at the Reuters Institute, states that tweeners, teens, and twenty-somethings look to "influencers" on social media not just for entertainment or advice, but also for cold, hard news.[5]

Double-edged Sword

The main issue I have with some citizen/independent journalists is that the qualities that make them effective – their intensity and fearlessness – can, if unchecked, also lead to a lack of comportment and a disregard for individual's rights. Also, as in the case of Aaron Mate, host/producer of The Grayzone, who was thrown off a train after he accosted Sen. Chris Coons, they tend to be overly-emotional and engage in advocacy journalism. Some of them may not have the proper training in journalism, and may not have been taught the rules of engagement. According to his LinkedIn profile, Mate earned a BA in Communications from Concordia University, located in Quebec, Canada, in 2003. This distinction likely means Mate underwent formal training in journalism, but may have also been inculcated by professors who preached advocacy and activism.[6]

Mate, whose Wikipedia entry identifies him as Jewish,[7] verbally ambushed Coons in a "quiet car" on a train, taking the side of the Palestinians following the massacre on October 7, 2023. There is an immediate disadvantage to this type of ambush journalism, because it immediately puts the source on the defensive, as opposed to a pre-arranged interview. But Mate was undeterred.

"Children are dying ... why not call for a cease (fire) ... they're being killed with our weapons," Mate said to Coons while sitting across from him and filming him.[8]

When Coons says, "Please stop talking to me," that should have ended the interview. Mate should have thanked him for his time and moved on. In most states, any further persistence could be construed as harassment. If Mate had stopped right there, he probably would not have been removed from the train at the next stop.

Coons even says to Mate at one point, "This is not professional journalism."[9]

Mate's journalistic process was ill-fated from the start because he began the interview by advocating for a particular side of an issue. If I had been conducting the interview, I might have asked for Coons' assessment of the current situation – an open-ended question that shows interest in the source's point of view – and then followed up with "Some experts say the U.S. should ask for an immediate cease-fire because American weapons are being used to harm thousands of children in Gaza. What are your thoughts on this?"

Those who hold public office and are effectively the stewards of taxpayers' money should be asked the tough questions, but the process should be one of professionalism, because that's how we would want to be treated. Every journalist is representing the craft as a whole. The reckless actions of a few reflect poorly on all journalists.

Leading the Way

Aside from Carlson, well-known anchors such as Don Lemon, Megyn Kelly, Bill O'Reilly, and Trish Regan have all left major networks and enjoyed success as independent journalists, parlaying their notoriety into new shows, subscription-based content, and other ventures.

James O'Keefe, the recently-martyred former face of Project Veritas – who first gained prominence for exposing the fraudulent ACORN[10] and ended his career at Veritas with an exposé of pharmaceutical giant Pfizer – has been proselytizing about citizen journalism for at least a decade.[11]

In a *Daily Northwestern* piece titled "Conservative activist James O'Keefe talks citizen journalism at 'Hating Breitbart' screening," published on May 14, 2013, and written by Patrick Svitek, O'Keefe addresses a crowd at Northwestern University while promoting a documentary about the late Andrew Breitbart.[12]

"I can't do it alone," O'Keefe told about 40 people in a Technological Institute auditorium. "They have come at me with everything. I'm still standing."[13]

It appears O'Keefe is implying that citizen journalism, free from political machinations and constricting corporate tentacles, can present news as it was meant to be, in its raw and unfiltered form. However, this also means that citizen journalists become targets of mainstream media and its supporters.

O'Keefe practiced his brand of reporting at Veritas for years before he was ousted in what some have described as an internal coup.[14] The organization banished O'Keefe, the founder and driving force of the organization, on allegations of embezzlement and violating its bylaws by firing the CFO without board approval.[15] There was a swift backlash by the public and Project Veritas' Twitter followers and YouTube subscribers plummeted.

But like the mythical phoenix, O'Keefe resurfaced, launching his own company, O'Keefe Media Group – OMG for short – to inject proverbial steroids into his model of citizen journalism.

"We are going to build an army of investigators and exposers," O'Keefe says in an OMG video. "They have awakened a sleeping giant."

In a news release, O'Keefe elaborates further, saying, "In the coming months you will see this army expanding across the country, every statehouse, every city council, every school board and everywhere people are conspiring to keep themselves in power, practice favoritism, or line their pockets with tax dollars."[16]

You might ask why I take activist journalists to task but spare O'Keefe, who has done his share of pursuing fleeing sources down city streets, hollering questions at them. I condemn all of it; every time it happens in an O'Keefe video, I cringe. I understand his penchant for hidden-camera gotcha stings, and although I never engaged in that as a reporter, the onus is on the target to watch what they say. But chasing someone down the street borders on harassment.

Another YouTuber who pioneered independent live streaming journalism is Tim Pool, whose main YouTube channel commands 1.65 million subscriptions. In 2011, armed with only a cell phone, sheer grit, and his now famous beard-and-beanie combo, Pool embedded himself in the crowds at Occupy Wall Street, a left-wing movement that described itself as "fighting back against the corrosive power of major banks and multinational corporations over the democratic process, and the role of Wall Street in creating an economic collapse that has caused the greatest recession in generations."[17]

While Pool may have initially been drawn to the movement out of curiosity and even camaraderie – press critic Jay Rosen described him as "clearly an activist and supporter of Occupy Wall Street as well as a reporter of it"[18] – Pool attributed his actions to curiosity, saying to John Stossel in an interview, "Some people don't trust the media, I don't know who to believe, why don't I just go there and I can see for myself?"[19]

According to one Redditor, Pool may have started out with moderate-to-left leanings, but is regarded as quasi-conservative now that the Democrats have been overtaken by radicals, according to some.

"Tim, like me and many others, has felt the ground shift beneath his feet. Back then (circa 2010) we had both left-wing and right-wing factions opposed to authoritarianism in government," wrote Redditor PugnansFidicen in 2022. "People like Tim and me are mostly no longer welcome on the left. Our views, once accepted or at least tolerated, are now considered heretical."[20]

Either way, Pool now finds himself accepted into conservative circles, as he was a panelist at AmericaFest 2023, along with host Charlie Kirk, where he discussed discovering woke culture.

"The first time I encountered the wokeness, whatever – Occupy Wall Street," Pool said. "Occupy actually created their organizational structure based around your race. They put all the black people in one group, all the Latinos, all the Asians..."

"I wonder why it fell apart," Kirk said.[21]

Making an Impact

The Twitter Files – as discussed in Chapter 8 – serve as two great journalism triumphs in one: A thrilling example of professional, unconstrained journalism and a media platform acknowledging past misconduct and pledging to do better in the future, a true rarity in media, social or otherwise.

Independent journalists have a powerful and passionate advocate in Musk, as he implied in a Twitter Spaces broadcast in November 2022 that legacy media previously had been given too much latitude on Twitter. In response, Musk is willing to harness the power of Twitter to elevate independent journalism.

"I think we will see articles (from) major newspapers where we know a lot about what actually happened, and what we know that what actually happened is not what is represented in that article," according to tweets by Sara Fischer. "I'm not saying we should somehow downplay the major publications or prominent journalists. I'm simply saying we should elevate people and give voice to the people. Much more."[22]

Beat Journalism

In my last few years as a reporter, I saw two defining characteristics of journalism slowly vanish. The first was the newsroom itself. Many brick-and-mortar newspaper buildings disappeared as a way to cut costs; the second was the concept of beat reporting. Typically, a reporter would specialize in a particular subject – crime, education, city government – so they could develop sources and immerse in the culture inside and out. But, as newsroom staffs were obliterated, less had to do more, and so beats were done away with; no specializing, everyone had to do every type of story and typically did, in the span of a day.

But it seems that some independent journalists have gravitated toward beat reporting.

YouTuber Peter Santanello travels the country, filming intense documentaries in intriguing locations with equally fascinating, yet often marginalized people. I would call what he does immersion journalism, or the human interest beat.

"I make videos showing you a world that the media fails to capture," Santanello states in his channel's description. "No BS polarization or political angle – just pure authentic interactions with the locals. I present the story. You present your own opinion."[23] That's beautiful, precisely what journalism should be.

Santanello's two videos from a trip to Appalachia garnered 3.5 and 2.2 million views, respectively, which is very impressive. He has also taken in-depth looks at Native American tribes, the housing projects in Watts, California, and the Chicano culture in East LA.

Now that's some true-blue journalism right there, folks.

Another guy producing similar content on YouTube, Tommy G, describes his channel with a simple, straightforward statement: "I make the craziest documentaries on YouTube." One of Tommy's most popular things to do is to document gang culture in such hotbeds as Chicago, Cincinnati, and Baltimore.[24]

On his YouTube channel's homepage, independent-investigative YouTuber Stephen "Coffeezilla" Findeisen describes his work as uncovering "scams, fraudsters and fake gurus that are preying on desperate people with deceptive advertising. If you have to ask... it's probably too good to be true."[25]

Findeisen's most prominent case to date is arguably his series examining an alleged crypto scam called CryptoZoo, developed and marketed by another YouTuber named Logan Paul. In his initial video on the case, Findeisen dissected why Paul's "really fun game that makes you money" was not fun for investors as they actually lost money.[26]

In the video, Findeisen exhibits many of the effective techniques of true journalism – he conducts extensive research on the CryptoZoo project, tracks down and interviews numerous victims, and considers that the game's developers may be partially to blame. Perhaps the crown jewel in the original video is Findeisen's attempt to allow Paul to explain his side of the story. Findeisen interviews Paul's manager, Jeff Levin, who initially stated he had no comment, but then continued talking, and so Findeisen kept recording. Then Levin issued a veiled legal threat.

"Your job as someone that is reporting news is to actually verify correct news."

"Right, that's why I'm calling you."

"I know and that's legal grounds for that stuff so I'm just telling you, legally, you have to report correct news with a verifiable information."

"Right, that's why I'm calling you," Findeisen says again.[27]

Andy Ngo gained notoriety not only for his live coverage of violent protests – which would fit into a crime or breaking news beat – in such urban war zones as Portland, Oregon, but also the alleged assaults he endured at the hands of several individuals in 2019, which he identified in civil court in 2023 as members of Antifa.

Ngo was seen by some as a tireless, unbiased journalist, although others, including EJ Dickson of *Rolling Stone* called him a "provocateur" and said he had a "long and rich history of trolling those on the left."[28]

Dickson went on to write that Ngo appeared to be in league with the Proud Boys and Patriot Prayer, two conservative counter-protest groups, which Ngo denied through his lawyer.[29]

But then Dickson engaged in some biased hyperbole about Ngo, stating, "He developed a knack for obtaining footage of anti-fascist protesters that leaned into preconceived notions of radical leftists, making them look violent, red-faced, angry, or even just irrational, a gimmick that landed him a handful of spots as a commentator on Fox News."[30] Making them look violent? How about displaying that they actually *are* violent? How would Ngo "make them look" anything by simply aiming a camera at them?

Ngo's lawyer, Dorothy Yamamoto, described her client as "merely an 'on-the-ground investigative journalist' that found a niche in covering political protests due to the lack of reporting by mainstream media during times of hyper-political polarization in the U.S." The attorney explained that the altercation with (John Colin) Hacker at a gym was the first time Ngo was confronted over his journalism work in a personal setting. She said that this was the moment Ngo "realized he was going to be recognized in public."[31]

In August 2023, three alleged Antifa members were found liable and ordered to pay Ngo $300,000 in damages for their role in the June 2019 "Milkshake Incident," when Ngo was physically assaulted – including getting blasted in the face with a milkshake – in Portland.[32]

Ngo reached a settlement with another alleged member on July 16, 2023, however details of the settlement were not available to the public. That left two other alleged members to stand trial.[33]

Ngo repeatedly jumped into the trenches with both feet to chronicle events that most mainstream journalists didn't have the guts to cover. Sure, there were journalists on the periphery of the rioting, but not many covered it to the degree of Ngo.

No Sell-outs

You start a company, you build it up, then you sell it to a corporation for lots of money. You might stay on in a leadership position, but you're no longer calling the shots. That's the normal progression of business; just ask Pat McAfee.

On May 17, 2023, on the Black and White Sports YouTube channel, hosts John Matrixx and Rhodes Rants dissected the recent move by McAfee, a former NFL punter/kicker-turned sports analyst who sold his independent show to sports kingpin ESPN.

Rhodes saw it as a frustrating moment in sports media, as highlighted by the importance of independent outlets, such as the one he operates with Matrixx, that exist outside of the mainstream media.

"One of the reasons why we watched the meteoric rise of the Pat McAfee Show is because he was the alternative to ESPN," Rhodes said. "We're in a different time in media where the actual public doesn't trust the media and we're looking for what's called citizen journalism to rise up and take ahold of society. The fact is, people don't trust ESPN, they don't trust Disney (ESPN's parent company) and so that's ... the value of the Pat McAfee Show."[34]

In early 2024, New York Jets quarterback Aaron Rodgers was pulled as a weekly guest from the McAfee show after the latest chapter of a long-running feud between Rodgers and ABC late night talk show host Jimmy Kimmel. On what was Rodgers' last episode of the show, he suggested that Kimmel was connected to sex trafficker and pedophile Jeffrey Epstein.[35] Here's what not everyone realizes – ESPN and ABC are both owned by Disney, so I'm sure it upset the powers-that-be that two entities under the same banner were squabbling.

"Some of his (Rodgers') thoughts and opinions, though, do piss off a lot of people," McAfee said after announcing Rodgers' ousting. "I'm pumped that that is no longer going to be every single Wednesday of my life, which it has been for the last few weeks."[36]

Had McAfee the outlaw still owned his show, Rodgers may have continued to be a guest without missing a beat. As it happened, Rodgers was on the show a day after McAfee made the announcement.[37]

And finally, it was independence that fueled Barstool Sports captain Dave Portnoy to buy back his company from Penn Entertainment for $1 three years after he sold it.

"We underestimated just how tough it is for myself and Barstool to operate in a regulated world," he said of the time after the sale. But upon buying it back, "For the first time in forever, we don't have to watch what we say, how we talk, what we do, it's back to the pirate ship … This is now going to be a place for content, content, content."[38]

Maybe McAfee could do the same one day.

---

[1] Bauder, David. "CNN Preaches Patience as Ratings Tank During Turnaround." AP News, March 30, 2023. https://apnews.com/article/cnn-ratings-chris-licht-584ea2b45819d2cc416006d7bd8b77e8.

[2] Fischer, Sara. "Twitter Press Suspensions Become Media Flashpoint." Axios, December 16, 2022. https://www.axios.com/2022/12/16/twitter-journalist-suspensions-media-elon-musk.

[3] Richard, Lawrence. "TikTok and Instagram Influencers Top List of Trusted News Sources for Today's Youth: Report." Fox News, June 14, 2023. https://www.foxnews.com/politics/tiktok-instagram-influencers-top-list-trusted-news-sources-todays-youth-report.

[4] Ibid.

[5] 336. HadiH. "Aaron Maté from TheGreyZone Confronts Sen. Chris Coons (D-Delaware) about His Support of IL Genocide." YouTube, November 13, 2023. https://www.youtube.com/watch?v=kAyNIZEJ65g.

6 Richard, Lawrence. "TikTok and Instagram Influencers Top List of Trusted News Sources for Today's Youth: Report." Fox News, June 14, 2023. https://www.foxnews.com/politics/tiktok-instagram-influencers-top-list-trusted-news-sources-todays-youth-report.

7 "Aaron Maté." Wikipedia, accessed March 31, 2024. https://en.wikipedia.org/wiki/Aaron_Mat%C3%A9.

8 HadiH. "Aaron Maté from TheGreyZone Confronts Sen. Chris Coons (D-Delaware) about His Support of IL Genocide." YouTube, November 13, 2023. https://www.youtube.com/watch?v=kAyNIZEJ65g.

9 Ibid.

10 Push Back Now. "Acorn Prostitution Investigation – James O'Keefe and Hannah Giles - Part 1." YouTube, September 10, 2009. https://www.youtube.com/watch?v=9UOL9Jh61S8.

11 The Hill. "Project Veritas New Video: Alleged Pfizer Scientist Caught Describing Mutating Viruses for Profit." YouTube, January 26, 2023. https://www.youtube.com/watch?v=7-LamoxBvWo.

12 Svitek, Patrick. "Conservative Activist James O'Keefe Talks Citizen Journalism at 'Hating Breitbart' Screening." *The Daily Northwestern*, May 14, 2013. https://dailynorthwestern.com/2013/05/14/campus/conservative-activist-james-okeefe-talks-citizen-journalism-at-hating-breitbart-screening/.

13 Ibid.

14 Phillips, Aleks. "Who Is Matthew Tyrmand? Project Veritas Board Member Under Scrutiny." *Newsweek*, February 21, 2023. https://www.newsweek.com/matthew-tyrmand-project-veritas-james-okeefe-1782681.

15 MacDonald, Cassandra. "Breaking: Project Veritas Board Releases Statement After Removing James O'Keefe and Losing over 100,000 Followers." The Gateway Pundit, February 20, 2023. https://www.thegatewaypundit.com/2023/02/breaking-project-veritas-board-releases-statement-after-removing-james-okeefe-and-losing-over-100000-followers/.

16 Hannity Staff. "OMG! O'Keefe Is Back! Ousted Project Veritas Founder Announces 'O'Keefe Media Group.'" Sean Hannity, March 15, 2023. https://hannity.com/media-room/omg-okeefe-is-back-ousted-project-veritas-founder-announces-okeefe-media-group/.

17 Occupy Wall Street. "About." Accessed March 31, 2024. http://occupywallst.org/about/.

18 Marantz, Andrew. "The Live-Streamers Who Are Challenging Traditional Journalism." *The New Yorker*, December 4, 2017.

https://www.newyorker.com/magazine/2017/12/11/the-live-streamers-who-are-challenging-traditional-journalism.

19 Stossel, John. "The Full Tim Pool: On Independent Reporting, Media Bias, Joe Rogan, Covington, & Protests. (Updated)." YouTube, October 13, 2022. https://www.youtube.com/watch?v=8iAXrw-lql0&t=1s.

20 R/Askconservatives on reddit: "How is Tim Pool a Liberal?" June 21, 2022. https://www.reddit.com/r/AskConservatives/comments/vhja7x/how_is_tim_pool_a_liberal/.

21 Turning Point Action. "Tim Pool Live at AmericaFest with Tucker Carlson and Charlie Kirk." YouTube, December 18, 2023. https://www.youtube.com/watch?v=bUQX7HWMTnY.

22 Fischer, Sara. "Musk's Feud with the Media Takes a Toll on Twitter." Axios, April 10, 2023. https://www.axios.com/2023/04/10/musk-twitter-media-feud.

23 "Peter Santenello." YouTube channel. Accessed March 31, 2024. https://www.youtube.com/@PeterSantenello/about.

24 "Tommy G." YouTube channel. Accessed March 31, 2024. https://www.youtube.com/@TommyGMcGee.

25 "Coffeezilla." YouTube channel, accessed March 31, 2024.

26 Coffeezilla. "Investigating Logan Paul's Biggest Scam." YouTube, December 16, 2022. https://www.youtube.com/watch?v=386p68_lDHA&t=1218s.

27 Ibid.

28 Dickson, EJ. "How a Right-Wing Troll Managed to Manipulate the Mainstream Media." *Rolling Stone*, September 3, 2019. https://www.rollingstone.com/culture/culture-features/andy-ngo-right-wing-troll-antifa-877914/.

29 Ibid.

30 Ibid.

31 Daviscourt, Katie. "Exclusive: Andy Ngo Faces Alleged Attackers in Portland Court for Day 1 of Civil Trial." The Post Millennial, August 2, 2023. https://thepostmillennial.com/exclusive-andy-ngo-faces-alleged-attackers-in-portland-court-for-day-1-of-civil-trial.

32 Daviscourt, Katie. "Breaking: Judge Rules Against Antifa Defendants in Default, Awards Andy NGO $300,000 in Damages over Portland Attack." The Post Millennial, August 22, 2023. https://thepostmillennial.com/breaking-judge-rules-against-antifa-defendants-in-default-awards-andy-ngo-300000-in-damages-over-portland-attack.

33 Daviscourt, Katie. "Exclusive: Andy Ngo Faces Alleged Attackers in Portland Court for Day 1 of Civil Trial." The Post Millennial, August 2, 2023. https://thepostmillennial.com/exclusive-andy-ngo-faces-alleged-attackers-in-portland-court-for-day-1-of-civil-trial.

34 Black and White Sports. "Pat McAfee Fans Destroy Him for Selling Out to Woke ESPN! He Goes Members Only on Livestream Chat!" YouTube, May 17, 2023. https://www.youtube.com/watch?v=SC9tbkVGCwE&t=2s.

35 Moreau, Jordan. "Aaron Rodgers Won't Return to 'The Pat McAfee Show' This Season After Jimmy Kimmel Feud: 'The Way It Ended, It Got Real Loud'." *Variety*, Jan. 10, 2024. https://variety.com/2024/tv/news/aaron-rodgers-leaves-pat-mcafee-jimmy-kimmel-1235867820/.

36 Ibid.

37 Rajagopalan, Rishikesh. "Aaron Rodgers appears on 'The Pat McAfee Show' day after supposed exit." CBSNews.com, Jan. 11, 2024. https://www.cbsnews.com/news/aaron-rodgers-pat-mcafee-appearance/.

38 Tangalakis-Lippert, Katherine, and Ashley Rodriguez. "Dave Portnoy Buys Barstool Sports Back for $1, Years after Selling It." Business Insider, August 8, 2023. https://www.businessinsider.com/dave-portnoy-buys-barstool-sports-back-penn-national-2023-8.

Chapter 15 – Local Ownership in News Deserts

In my 25 years as a reporter, I witnessed local news deteriorate from front-page stories to being effectively ignored. The paper had a group of freelance writers to cover municipal meetings, but it seemed the money for them dried up and so staffers would only report on the major government news around the county.

Sadly, this was to the overall detriment of the newspaper industry. Why? Well, as the saying goes, never forget where you came from. Journalism starts at the local level. If you are dependent on those who live around you to buy your product, your product must resonate with them. You must create and maintain an emotional connection with them. It almost has to act like a mirror and reflect back to them who and what they are. If a paper contains just a couple local stories and then a bunch of national news items, people might not think it's worth buying. They can get their national news elsewhere, possibly for free, so why would they pay to get it from you?

Local news – not just municipal meetings, but crime, sports, and human interest – was and should continue to be the foundation of small and regional newspapers. But if you take a sledgehammer to the foundation, pretty soon the rest will crumble.

Let's take a look at what a little paper in Virginia did to stay alive. *The Recorder*, from what Anne Adams, owner, publisher and editor of the paper, can tell, is woven into the fabric of the community. It was featured on a Judy Woodruff story on PBS News Hour titled "The connections between decline of news and growing political division."[1]

"*The Recorder* has helped hold this community with its long, proud history together for 146 years," Woodruff said. "It's done so mainly by selling ads and subscriptions at a time when so many local newspapers across the country have collapsed."[2]

Adams said the paper's readers don't hold back when the paper has "crossed the line." She, in turn, feels it is her duty to get to the bottom of the news in the three counties the paper serves and present readers with the right information, which in turn, keeps them involved in their communities.[3]

According to the story, in 2017, Adams increased the newsstand price of the paper by more than 100 percent, from $2 to $5. "And it was just five issues away from folding during the pandemic when its readers stepped in with donations to keep the presses going," Woodruff said.[4]

In South Carolina, *The Charleston Post* and *Courier* owner Pierre Manigault insists that newspapers have to get back to the "roots" of journalism – content they can't find anywhere else. "If you do that, people will care ... with their hearts and their wallets," he told Ted Koppel in a *CBS Sunday Morning* segment in 2023.[5]

Instead of increasing the price of the paper as Adams did, Manigault devised a different method of financial support from the community – a donation drive.

"Well, we opened up a fund through the community foundation where people could pay for the newsroom expenses associated with our investigative journalism," Manigault said. "We set a goal of $100,000 in 100 days. And we raised about five times that."[6]

In the next part of this book, I caution against media outlets accepting donations from outside interests. In the case of *The Charleston Post* and *Courier*, I make an exception, because the donations are emanating from members of the public, not government or other companies or organizations. If the intentions of the public are to see the paper survive and continue to provide quality news, I support that wholeheartedly.

Returning to local news coverage is one prong of success for newspapers; the other is that these papers need to be owned by someone with deep pockets who already lives in the community. Local owners have a stake in their communities; they care about what goes on there. They know the people who are their readers. They serve them and often write about them. They have to look them in the eye. The only choke point is that the paper must operate in an autonomous capacity from its owner. One possible solution would be to establish a board of directors, which would serve to govern the paper's policies and procedures and to ensure the owner remains excluded from how the paper is run. This entire scenario could be applied to the ownership of a local TV station as well.

Let's take a look at a recent survey, "American Views: Trust, Media and Democracy, Part 2," coordinated by the Gallup/Knight Foundation and published in February 2023.[7] The poll begins with the premise that a democracy is incumbent upon, among other things, a strong media. In order to have a strong media, there has to be trust between it and the public. And the highest, strongest form of trust is what they call "emotional trust."[8]

"The new survey of about 5,600 Americans demonstrates that more than twice as many Americans have higher emotional trust in local news than in national news," according to the survey.[9]

And if there is higher emotional trust, then more than likely that will lead to an increased willingness to pay for news.

"Higher emotional trust in local news is related to a higher likelihood of having paid for news and willingness to do so in the future," the survey states.[10]

In a real-world example, in 2019, Gannett merged with GateHouse, making it the largest chain in the U.S. Two years later, a story on Northwestern University's website, Local News Initiative, reported on the trend of Gannett selling off smaller papers.

"After decades of consolidation in local news ownership, we could be on the cusp of a back-to-the-future moment with more local operators, especially in smaller communities," said Tim Franklin, Senior Associate Dean, and John M. Mutz Chair in Local News at Medill, according to the Northwestern story.[11]

And then we have a March 28, 2023 story from Axios that has more details, straight from the CEO's mouth.

"More newspaper sales could be on the way for Gannett, which has lost roughly half of its workforce since merging with GateHouse ... Gannett's strategy in the wake of the merger has been to shed assets and focus on fewer, more lucrative, markets. CEO Mike Reed said on last month's earnings call that the company 'would entertain bids on any of our markets.'"[12]

As of the story's publishing, Gannett had about 217 daily newspapers, and Reed said that with future sell-offs, the chain was targeting a number somewhere between that and its top 100 papers.[13]

And while Gannett has tried to focus on selling its smaller and lower-performing papers, sometimes they have simply closed them, leaving what are known as "news deserts."[14]

In an NPR story written by Manuela López Restrepo, journalist Joshua Benton states that other journalists have taken up the mantle of providing local news coverage in smaller communities.[15]

"There are communities across the country where smart digital outlets are growing to the point where in some cases, they have bigger newsrooms than the local daily newspaper does. It is possible, but it's a challenge," he said.[16]

Here's a great example of exactly what they're talking about. In 2018, Davis Shaver launched an independent media website called LebTown, which covers Lebanon County, Pennsylvania.

"The site has grown since then from an occasional Lebanon-focused blog into a full-fledged news organization," according to its website. "Today it is arguably the 'paper of record' for Lebanon County and reaches on average more than 100,000 readers monthly."[17]

It turned out to be a brilliant move by Shaver. The incumbent paper, the *Lebanon Daily News*, is owned by Gannett, and I can tell you at least when I was there, the staff was pared down to one or two reporters. That means you're probably producing four new local stories per day, at best. The rest of the "news hole" was filled with wire stories from Gannett's *USAToday* Network and then other stories from the surrounding area, like York, Hanover, and Chambersburg. But here's the problem – very few people in Lebanon care about what's going on in York, Hanover, or Chambersburg. They want to hear about what's going on in their backyard.

The fallout from the dastardly deeds wrought by the media in the first section was as varied and organic as it was significant.

I don't know that anyone could have predicted that the consequences to an out-of-control media would have manifested it the form of two major figures in Trump and Musk. What should have been expected was the nosedive of readership and viewership, which then begat layoffs to recoup losses. However, the perpetual swirling vortex was then entered: Fewer staff = less quality work = fewer customers = lay-offs, rinse and repeat. On the positive side, we saw the emergence of independent/citizen journalists and what appears to be a resurgence of local ownership with a focus on local news.

Buckle up, we have one more section to go, possibly the most important.

---

[1] Woodruff, Judy, et al. "The Connections between Decline of Local News and Growing Political Division." PBS, August 30, 2023. https://www.pbs.org/newshour/show/the-connections-between-decline-of-local-news-and-growing-political-division.

[2] Ibid.

[3] Ibid.

[4] Ibid.

[5] Koppel, Ted. "Extra! New Strategies for Survival by South Carolina Newspapers." CBS News, July 2, 2023. https://www.cbsnews.com/news/the-uncovered-project-and-the-survival-of-south-carolina-newspapers/.

[6] Ibid.

[7] "Gallup/Knight Study Offers New Insights on Why Americans' Trust in News Continues to Decline." Knight Foundation, February 15, 2023. https://knightfoundation.org/press/releases/gallup-knight-study-offers-new-insights-on-why-americans-trust-in-news-continues-to-decline/.

[8] Ibid.

[9] Ibid.

[10] Ibid.

[11] Jacob, Mark. "News Unchained: More Outlets Going Back to Local Ownership." Local News Initiative, July 26, 2021.

https://localnewsinitiative.northwestern.edu/posts/2021/07/26/increasing-local-ownership/.

[12] Fischer, Sara. "Gannett CEO Forecasts More Daily Newspaper Sales." Axios, March 28, 2023. https://www.axios.com/2023/03/28/gannett-ceo-talks-future-sales.

[13] Ibid.

[14] Fuller, Jason, et al. "The Fate of Local News: America's Largest Newspaper Company Is Creating News Deserts." NPR, April 6, 2023. https://www.npr.org/2023/04/06/1168488156/the-fate-of-local-news-americas-largest-newspaper-company-is-creating-news-deser.

[15] Fuller, Jason, et al. "The Fate of Local News: America's Largest Newspaper Company Is Creating News Deserts." NPR, April 6, 2023. https://www.npr.org/2023/04/06/1168488156/the-fate-of-local-news-americas-largest-newspaper-company-is-creating-news-deser.

[16] Ibid.

[17] "We're Here to Help Make Lebanon County a Better Place." LebTown, March 16, 2024. https://lebtown.com/about/.

PART 3

RECKONING

Chapter 16 – The Other Way Doesn't Work

To me, there is nothing more frustrating than reading a book or article or watching a video where there's someone – say a Negative Nancy or a Depressed Donny – dishing out disparaging remarks about an issue, but then they never propose what they think should be done to improve it. That's really the other half of the equation; you can't just leave people hanging, it's disingenuous.

So in this part of the book, I'm going to intimate some ways that I believe this whole big mess can be turned around. Of course, I want you to read to the end – but spoiler alert – what it truly comes down to is a return to *the way things were*. You can call me old-fashioned, say I'm resisting "change." And you know what? You're right.

Change that contradicts the tenets of true journalism is doomed to fail. We now see the disastrous results of the experiment – distrust and even hatred of the mainstream media. The pendulum was somehow allowed to swing into a nebulous world of worshipping false gods of activism, elitism, and authoritarianism.

The American media needs a return to hard-boiled, objective, old-school journalism. I truly believe it is the only way the media will capture the hearts and minds of the majority of the American public and possibly start making money again. The alternative is the media continues to sink into the abyss of partisan, payola-taking patheticism until it hemorrhages itself out of existence. And maybe a new breed that adopts the ideals of true journalism will become the mainstream. It may be happening right now, as outlined in Chapter 14.

In a story on the popular grassroots conservative website Gateway Pundit, veteran cable commentator Larry Johnson discusses the seismic shift in American journalism that is occurring in a story titled "Is the Mainstream Media a Relic of the Past?"[1]

First, Johnson makes the point that despite the U.S. population increase over the decades, overall viewership of mainstream news outlets is down, from 53 million in 1968, with a population of 200 million, to 28 million in 2016, with a population of 323.1 million, according to the U.S. Census Bureau.[2]

Johnson recalls a time when he would go on-air to do "hit" – a short segment with a host and other guests – and there would be a relatively respectful exchange of ideas and opinions. He began to notice a widening of the political chasm between cable networks in 2008.[3]

"Fox became the anti-Obama channel and the rest of the media donned their Obama cheerleading outfits," Johnson writes. "The age of honest debate (if it ever existed) was over."[4]

Johnson submits that the rise of the digital age has brought with it a multitude of possibilities for dispersing and digesting the news.[5]

"We cannot (and should not) go back to the halcyon days of the 1990s and early 2000s," he writes. "The combination of blogs and podcasts have created a new world that cuts across international borders and provides the means for creating a genuine international community of conversation. We just have to do what we can."[6]

Johnson is right; we're at the point where most people gravitate to their respective echo-chambers to reaffirm what they already believe. The major media outlets are either on one side of the political aisle or the other. Is it possible to return to a time where people tune into the news for the news and not simply to have their views reflected back to them?

---

[1] Johnson, Larry. "Is the Mainstream Media a Relic of the Past?" The Gateway Pundit, August 28, 2023.
https://www.thegatewaypundit.com/2023/08/is-mainstream-media-relic-past/.

[2] Ibid.

[3] Ibid.

[4] Ibid.

[5] Ibid.

[6] Ibid.

Chapter 17 – Mea Culpas

Some might call it drastic. Or unnecessary. Or even ridiculous.

But just think about it: America loves a comeback. It's one of the great Hollywood stories we never tire of, but it's so much sweeter when it happens in real life... and then Hollywood screws the story up when they make a movie about it.

What am I talking about? It's time for the media to apologize to the American people for decades of irresponsible journalism.

There have been a few notable apologies from both network TV and newspapers over the years, but those have been in response to specific mistakes that were made by certain outlets. What I have in mind is an overarching, all-encompassing apology, something like this:

> "Over the years, possibly over many decades, we as a news outlet let you, our readers (viewers), down. We succumbed to outside pressure. We accepted gifts, money or otherwise, from groups and organizations that, either implied or outright requested we quash a story we planned to publish or concoct a story that contained untruths. We at times allowed agencies or individuals within the government to influence the direction we took on stories. Internally, we as journalists became susceptible to political ideologies that were then reflected in our work. To that end, we abandoned the pillars of journalism – to be fair, timely, thorough, and objective – as much as is humanly possible. For all of these, and many more not mentioned

herein, we sincerely apologize and ask for the American people to forgive us. We solemnly swear to wholeheartedly improve our journalistic processes and to return to journalism as it was meant to be – without political bias, without smear, without untruths. From this day forward, we will report stories with fairness and objectivity and let you, the reader (viewer), construct your own opinion, rather than telling you what and how to think. Thank you."

That's a start, but here's something to keep in mind. The chunk of readers and viewers who have checked out will not be reached by a message like this on your platform – because they've left it! So I would suggest a series of town hall meetings around the country in key markets. Really get down to the grass-roots level of things, sending an emissary to look people in the eye and tell them you screwed up and that you will do better. This emissary will need a non-confrontational demeanor yet possess extra-thick skin so they are not easily rattled – because they're going to be at the business-end of it! You're not going to convince everyone to give you a shot, but if you get them in the door, there's a chance you can sway some of them. Then arrange for local news outlets in TV, print, and online, both legacy and independent/citizen, to cover the town halls.

Although it wasn't an apology *per se*, CNN seemed to capture the spirit of one in 2022 that broke from their legendary left-leaning proclivities when newly-hired Chris Licht and David Zaslav talked about giving Republicans a fair shake on the network.[1] Convening the Trump Town Hall was the first major step, but then instead of holding fast and building on the momentum, they caved to outside pressure, and a dip in viewership ensued. The answer to detractors like Amanpour and Darcy should have been, "Look, this is the new direction we're headed. We feel it's the right one and we hope you will too. Expect to see more examples of it in the future." Licht was fired about a month after the Trump Town Hall, signifying a possible return to a liberal status quo for the network.

The first step for the media is to apologize, but the second step is equally, if not more important: To execute their promises and to adhere to them permanently. Keep doing it over and over again until it becomes natural, until it is woven into the fabric of the processes of news gathering and distribution. But it takes discipline. It's fine to be motivated, but motivation is emotion-driven, so it can be fleeting. That's when discipline takes over. Discipline is that internal voice that drives you to do something when you don't want to do it, because you know it must be done. So journalism needs true mavericks, stalwarts at the helm to persevere in the face of adversity, because there's going to be plenty of push-back.

But would the American consumer be convinced at hearing an apology such as the one I suggested? I suspect there's a large segment of the population that would be very forgiving, one portion that is gone forever, and one portion that would be in a "wait and see" mode.

I'm not the only one with the idea of a media *mea culpa*. Former Republican Presidential candidate Vivek Ramaswamy, in a conversation with several reporters, including an NBC reporter, also suggested the media formally apologize to the American public for perpetuating false narratives about the Hunter Biden laptop story, the origin of COVID-19 virus, and the Trump-Russia collusion hoax. Note: I already had my idea on this fleshed out before I watched the video with Ramaswamy.

"I'm still waiting for one honest anchor in the mainstream media to just look their own audience in the eye and say 'Hey, I apologize. We lied to you, we got it wrong and we'll never have this happen again,'" Ramaswamy said. "I think we need to use every occasion we have, to at least rebuild trust with the American public to say, 'Here's the narrative we set, here's where we were proven wrong, and here's where we own accountability."[2]

YouTuber Doug in Exile agreed that such a scenario would need to occur to repair the damage that has been wrought, but he was pessimistic that it would ever materialize. "You're not going to get an apology, you're not going to get a *mea culpa*, which is what the media would have to do for us to start trusting them again."[3]

If not a sweeping apology, admitting you were wrong on a case-by-case basis, in a swift and decisive manner, is the next best thing. We witnessed two examples of that in 2023.

In August 2023, on a CNN broadcast with host Jake Tapper and correspondent Jeff Zeleny, Tapper referenced a story written by *The Washington Post*'s Glenn Kessler titled "Biden said his son earned no money from China. His son says otherwise."[4]

Tapper then references Kessler's story about Hunter Biden reporting that he earned nearly $2.4 million in 2017 and $2.2 million in 2018, most of which was disbursed to him by Chinese and Ukrainian sources.[5]

"I mean, Trump was right," Tapper said. "I mean, he (Hunter) did make a fortune from China and Joe Biden was wrong. I don't know that he was lying about it, he might not have been told by Hunter, but this blind spot is a problem."[6]

Hold it right there. Did longtime anti-Trumper Jake Tapper just utter the words "Trump was right"? Zeleny also appeared to pull back the curtain a bit by implying that the Biden campaign does not want reporters asking about Hunter Biden. But think about it – since when is CNN critical of the Bidens? "But is there a blind spot directly around him and the campaign by not talking about this?" Zeleny said. "It's verboten. You can't talk about Hunter Biden. We'll see. This is definitely going to be a topic on the debate stage this week."7

Moving on to the newspaper known as the Old Gray Lady, in what is most likely a rare moment of introspection and clarity, another longtime anti-Trumper, *The New York Times*' David Brooks, wrote a column on Aug. 2, 2023 titled "What if we're the bad guys here?" which immediately brings to mind the clip from BBC comedy *That Mitchell and Webb Look* where one particularly pensive Nazi says to another, "Hans, are we the baddies?"8

Brooks explains that he and others, as part of the cultural elites, have designed and instituted the systems that oppress those less fortunate, essentially creating a class warfare scenario in America and effectively paving the way for a political messiah like Trump.

"Armed with all kinds of economic, cultural and political power, we support policies that help ourselves," he writes. "Like all elites, we use language and mores as tools to recognize one another and exclude others … We also change the moral norms in ways that suit ourselves, never mind the cost to others."9

Fantastic, but then Brooks snaps himself back in lock-step with leftist cognitive dissonance. He says he still trusts the American criminal justice system, but in the same breath says, "Trump is a monster in the way we've all been saying for years and deserves to go to prison." Right, so with no proof and no due process for Trump, just toss him in the clink straightaway. Got it.

These moments from Tapper and Brooks are significant, and we can only hope for more of them, so that anomaly becomes regularity. I'm not holding my breath, though.

A final thought on the apology – it would be so shocking, but it just might work. If a news network broadcasted it on prime time or a newspaper positioned it across the top of its front page, that would garner coverage across the globe and might even trigger other news outlets to follow suit. When you look at everything laid out in this book, the state of journalism is a dire one, so what do you have to lose?

---

[1] Reich, Robert. "The Changes at CNN Look Politically Motivated. That Should Concern Us All." *The Guardian*, August 24, 2022. https://www.theguardian.com/commentisfree/2022/aug/24/the-changes-at-cnn-look-politically-motivated-that-should-concern-us-all.

[2] Mr Producer Media. "Vivek Ramaswamy Calls out Mainstream Media Lies." Rumble, January 2, 2024. https://rumble.com/v44rdsr-vivek-ramaswamy-calls-out-mainstream-media-lies.html.

[3] Doug In Exile. "Vivek Ends NBC in Public." YouTube, January 2, 2024. https://www.youtube.com/watch?v=Vbbzhzyn7R4.

[4] Kessler, Glen. "Biden Said His Son Earned No Money from China. His Son Says Otherwise." *The Washington Post*, August 1, 2023. https://www.washingtonpost.com/politics/2023/08/01/biden-said-his-son-earned-no-money-china-his-son-says-otherwise/.

[5] Ibid.

[6] Ibid.

[7] Kaloi, Stephanie. "CNN's Jake Tapper: 'Trump Was Right' About Hunter Biden's Foreign Income (Video)." TheWrap, August 19, 2023. https://www.thewrap.com/cnn-jake-tapper-donald-trump-was-right-hunter-biden-foreign-income/.

[8] CrystalRoseCreations. "Mitchell and Webb: 'Are We the Baddies?'" YouTube, June 1, 2013. https://www.youtube.com/watch?v=ToKcmnrE5oY.

[9] Brooks, David. "What If We're the Bad Guys Here?" *The New York Times*, August 2, 2023. https://www.nytimes.com/2023/08/02/opinion/trump-meritocracy-educated.html.

Chapter 18 – Do the Work

The media issuing an apology for decades of deception might be enough for some, but for many others, it won't be enough. Once the apology is given, now comes the hard part – following through.

Let the Public Think for Itself

Following its Trump Town Hall, CNN held another town hall with Republican Presidential candidate Vivek Ramaswamy on Dec. 13, 2023, this time with anchor Abby Phillip as host. The conversation turned adversarial between Ramaswamy and Phillip when he broached the subject of what he believed was a government "that has lied to us systematically over the last several years" about the origin of COVID-19, about the Hunter Biden laptop, Trump-Russia disinformation hoax, and the presence and role of federal agents in the crowd during the January 6th protest at the Capitol.[1]

Phillip interjected and filibustered Ramaswamy when he brought up circumstantial evidence to suggest that there may be more to Jan. 6, which some refer to as the "fedsurrection," than was originally reported. Ramaswamy stated several inconvenient truths of that day, including undercover federal agents in the crowd, rubber bullets, and tear gas fired at protesters, and that 200 hours of footage were withheld throughout the convening of the Jan. 6th commission.[2]

Then, when Ramaswamy brought up the plot to kidnap Michigan Gov. Gretchen Whitmer – and that the entire scheme may have been designed to entrap a group of individuals by the federal government – Phillip went on the offensive again saying, "I don't want to have to interrupt you, I really don't, but I don't want you to mislead the audience here."[3] Her point was that there were some defendants who were found guilty. Ramaswamy had said three were acquitted.

I'm not saying that media hosts shouldn't challenge guests, but similar to the Trump Town Hall, allow the person you are interviewing the space to express himself. It's a main tenet of true journalism. People are tuning in and filling the seats in the audience because they want to hear the man talk, so let him talk. If you advertised it without him, you probably wouldn't have had an audience. Let him have his say, then clarify and push back all you want. But don't forcefully and continuously interrupt him. The people need to make up their own minds, but they won't be able to do that if the man is not allowed to utter even one complete sentence. Again, this is the media pushing a narrative and telling its audience what to think, rather than allowing them to make up their own minds. They're smarter than you think they are. It's very demeaning and unprofessional.

The media should not be in the business of burying, delaying, or omitting stories, like the Hunter Biden laptop story. Don't rewrite or fabricate history, like the 1619 Project. Cover news as it happens and cover it with integrity. Don't take sides. Everyone is fair game.

Apologizing means nothing without putting it into action. That means we have to have everyone – reporters, editors, managers, owners – grow a spine and rebuke anyone who criticizes true journalism. Report the news as it is and as it is happening.

Write It Straight

In *Monty Python and the Holy Grail*, the Knights of Ni are a fearsome group, but they have a weakness: The word "It." Their leader, who stands about twice as tall as the others, screeches at one point, "Don't say the word!"[4]

That's how I envisioned the mainstream media's reaction to Trump using the word "bloodbath" during a speech in March 2024 about the auto industries of U.S.-Mexico-China and what would happen if he were not elected to office. The media seized on the word and acted as if it were the most vile, reprehensible utterance ever created. But many said the media took Trump's use of the word out of context and weaponized it in a fiendish plot to derail his Presidential campaign. Mainstream media outlets lost their sense of literal vs. figurative and interpreted Trump's phrase as if they were a petulant five-year-old.

Here is Trump's full quote from his March 16, 2024 speech:

> "Mexico has taken, over a period of 30 years, 34 percent of the automobile manufacturing business in our country. Think of it, went to Mexico. China now, is building a couple of massive plants, where they're going to build the cars in Mexico and think, they think, that they're going to sell those cars into the United States, with no tax at the border. Let me tell you something to China, if you're listening President Xi – and you and I are friends but he understands the way I deal – those big, monster, car manufacturing plants that you're building in Mexico right now, and you think you're going to get that, you're going to not hire Americans and you're going to sell the cars to us, no, we're going to put a 100 percent tariff on every single car that comes across the line, and you're not going to be able to sell those cars. If I get elected. Now if I don't get elected, it's going

to be a bloodbath for the whole ... that's going to be the least of it, it's going to be a bloodbath for the country, that'll be the least of it. But they're not going to sell those cars, they're building massive factories."[5]

The media took the bait. Take a look at these YouTube headlines:

NBC's Today show: "Trump says there will be a 'bloodbath' if he isn't reelected."[6]

MSNBC: "David Corn slams Trump's claim of a 'bloodbath' if he loses presidential election."[7]

ABC: "Trump warns: 'If I don't get elected, it's going to be a bloodbath'."[8]

The Telegraph: "Donald Trump warns of 'bloodbath' if he loses presidential election."[9]

As to be expected, CNN gave longtime Trump nemesis and former Speaker of the House Nancy Pelosi a substantial platform and she used it to advance the bloodbath narrative.

"He's even predicting a bloodbath, what does that mean?" she said. "He's going to exact a bloodbath? There's something wrong here."[10]

Apparently if you're Trump, you can't say "bloodbath."

But, if you're He Xiaopeng, CEO of EV maker Xpeng, you sure can. "This year also marks the beginning of a fierce competition that may end in a 'bloodbath' (or as I prefer to call it, the brutal 'knockout round') among Chinese auto makers," Xiaopeng wrote in the employee memo.[11]

In 2020, Joe Biden also used the term when discussing Democrat in-fighting that threatened to make the party susceptible to a Trump victory: "What we can't let happen is let this primary become a negative bloodbath," Biden told more than 100 donors gathered at a private residence in Bethesda.[12]

X user Tom Elliott posted a "Bloodbath supercut" highlight video of numerous mainstream media talking heads – including Rachel Maddow, Erin Burnett, Charles Blow, and Van Jones – using "bloodbath" long before Trump. One of them used the term three times in one sentence![13]

All that said, when it comes to news, the American public is not hard to please. Just play it straight, deliver the unvarnished information as accurately as possible – no agendas, no narratives – and get the heck out of the way so they can make up their own minds.

It sounds simple, but it's the execution that will be a formidable opponent for the mainstream media. Let's take the issue of immigration. President Biden's White House adopted a "catch and release" program not seen during the preceding Trump administration. When border agents catch anyone crossing into the country illegally, they are not forced to return to their home country, but are released into the U.S. to await adjudication,[14] which, according to the AP, could take as much as a decade.[15]

When University of Georgia nursing student Laken Riley, 22, was allegedly attacked and killed on Feb. 22, 2024, by illegal alien Venezuelan Jose Antonio Ibarra, 26, the mainstream media appeared to sow subterfuge on the subject by not describing him as a non-citizen or reporting his prior criminal record. Why, in this case, would they do such a thing? Was it to distract from the notion that had Ibarra not entered the U.S. illegally and had not been allowed to remain in the country after racking up criminal charges,[16] including child endangerment, Laken would still be alive? With the Presidential campaign building, and the media knowing immigration would be a major issue, they appeared to crank up their propaganda machine. To quote a famous song, there's no valley low enough...[17]

The AP's headline, "The killing of a nursing student out for a run highlights the fears of solo female athletes," seems to blame Laken, that she had somehow invited her attack by running alone. The body of the story was no better, referring to Ibarra as "Athens resident" – can you be a true resident if you are in the U.S. illegally? – while completely omitting his criminal record.[18]

Then there was the *Post*'s headline, "Migrant charged with murdering Laken Riley likely panicked when she fought back."[19] The *Post*'s reputation is one of being fierce and fearless, but this time a flunkie must have been in charge of the editorial desk to let this one get through. This is victim-blaming of the highest order. I can tell you from experience this is a common practice; journalists interview subject-matter experts about a particular incident and although they are knowledgeable, they truly don't know any more than we do, yet they are expected to connect dots and make sweeping generalizations. The way I read the headline, the profiler is asserting that had Laken not fought back, Ibarra may not have panicked, and that if he hadn't panicked, he might not have killed her, so it's her fault she's dead.

It appears the *Post* later changed the headline to "Nursing student Laken Riley tried to call 911 before deadly encounter with migrant" but only after taking considerable heat online.[20] But they kept the line in the story – "Ibarra then panicked and likely bashed in her skull when Riley bravely tried to fight back, according to an analysis by a former criminal profiler," and then followed with a quote from the profiler, "He's (Ibarra) not a very big fellow and he may have been overwhelmed by her size and her strengths and tenacity to fight back," which makes it seem like had Laken been smaller, he would not have been "forced" to kill her.

Don't Be a Sucker

Ten days after the Hamas terrorist attack on Israel on Oct. 7, 2023, several major media outlets – including the Associated Press, *The New York Times, Wall Street Journal*, and the BBC – appeared to blindly advance the narrative that Israel launched a missile at a West Bank hospital, killing nearly 500 people.

As it turned out, none of that was true. The missile on Oct. 17, 2023, did not come from Israel, but was a misfire from a Palestinian Islamic jihad group; it didn't strike the hospital, but a nearby parking lot; therefore, the death toll was significantly lower.[21]

The erroneous information about the bombing was disseminated to the media by Gaza's Health Ministry, which, similar to other societal systems in Gaza, is controlled by Hamas.[22]

It doesn't take a reporter to figure out that information from one side of the conflict should be closely vetted, because, well, they have a personal stake in it, so of course they would want to cast their side in a positive light and besmirch the opposition.

I honestly don't know if the legacy media was plain dumb, lazy, or simply hell-bent on pushing a puzzling agenda of protecting Hamas while painting the Israelis as evil to the core. Or maybe their thirst to be first blinded them. Yet another tenet in journalism is that you have to be first and accurate; first and wrong doesn't count.

As the evidence from the Israelis – yes, they are on the other side, but they provided concrete evidence – reached a fever pitch, *The New York Times* fell on its proverbial sword on Oct. 23, 2023, admitting it mishandled the coverage of the bombing.

"The early versions of the coverage – and the prominence it received in a headline, news alert and social media channels – relied too heavily on claims by Hamas, and did not make clear that those claims could not immediately be verified. The report left readers with an incorrect impression about what was known and how credible the account was … *Times* editors should have taken more care with the initial presentation, and been more explicit about what information could be verified."[23]

Let me get this straight. They knew the information was coming from a terrorist organization and they knew the claims were not verified, but they went ahead and published it anyway? Reprehensible.

A lengthy CNN.com story included a correction about their reporting *waaay* down at the bottom – I think corrections should go at the top, by the way – that read:

"CORRECTION: This article on the Gaza hospital blast initially did not clearly attribute claims about Israel's responsibility to the Hamas-controlled Ministry of Health in Gaza. Israel later said a 'misfired' rocket by militant group Islamic Jihad caused the blast and produced evidence to support its claim. U.S. President Joe Biden said the Israeli position is backed by U.S. intelligence. CNN's forensic analysis of images and videos suggests a rocket fired from within Gaza caused the blast, not an Israeli airstrike. An earlier version of this story also misidentified the embassy protesters attempted to reach in Amman. It was the Israeli embassy."[24]

The BBC on Oct. 19, 2023, issued a clarification over their coverage of the bombing, as evidenced by an *Independent* headline that read, "BBC News deputy CEO admits 'mistake' in live coverage of Gaza hospital bombing."[25]

Jonathan Munro, deputy chief executive of the BBC, stated, "The correspondent (Jon Donnison) was wrong to speculate about the cause of the explosion of the hospital. At no stage did he actually say it was caused by the Israelis... but nonetheless, when the impression is left that we've speculated, (it) is important to correct that which we've done."[26]

The positive of all this is the media admitted they committed significant journalistic errors, but had they engaged in some due diligence, it could have been avoided. The bottom line is that the media should not advocate for one side over another of the Israelis versus the Palestinians. It appears the media was looking for a villain and somehow decided it was the Israelis, despite the initial attack perpetrated by Hamas.

---

[1] CNN. "Abby Phillip Fact-Checks Vivek Ramaswamy on Conspiracy Theory." YouTube, December 13, 2023. https://www.youtube.com/watch?v=PnMs9358nVU&t=7s.

[2] Ibid.

[3] Ibid.

[4] Ferry, Kenny. "The Knights of Ni Finally Get Their Shrubbery." YouTube, June 12, 2010. https://www.youtube.com/watch?v=RZvsGdJP3ng.

[5] Payne, Ed. "Fact Check: Trump Used the Word 'Bloodbath' in Car Import Tariff Segment of Speech." Lead Stories, March 18, 2024. https://leadstories.com/hoax-alert/2024/03/fact-check-trump-used-the-word-bloodbath-in-car-import-tarriff-segment-of-speech.html.

[6] Today. "Trump Says There Will Be a 'Bloodbath' If He Isn't Reelected." YouTube, March 17, 2024. https://www.youtube.com/watch?v=7LEPMEg20Ck.

[7] MSNBC. "David Corn Slams Trump's Claim of a 'Bloodbath' If He Loses Presidential Election." YouTube, March 17, 2024. https://www.youtube.com/watch?v=s7RdAufkLkk.

8 ABC News. "Trump Warns: 'If I Don't Get Elected, It's Going to Be a Bloodbath.'" YouTube, March 17, 2024. https://www.youtube.com/watch?v=Lokw_nsumD0.

9 The Telegraph. "Donald Trump Warns of 'Bloodbath' If He Loses Presidential Election." YouTube, March 17, 2024. https://www.youtube.com/watch?v=Qh8HqfBJXiA.

10 The Hill. "Bloodbath Prediction? Nancy Pelosi, Media Smears Trump over Auto Worker Comments." YouTube, March 18, 2024. https://www.youtube.com/watch?v=vUZpOP1PrTI.

11 Kharpal, Arjun. "Xpeng Plans to Hire 4,000 People, Invest in AI as CEO Warns Intense EV Rivalry May End in 'Bloodbath.'" CNBC, February 19, 2024. https://www.cnbc.com/2024/02/19/xpeng-plans-to-hire-4000-people-invest-in-ai.html.

12 Korecki, Natasha. "Biden's 'Bernie Brothers' Remark Lights Up Social Media." Politico, March 6, 2020. https://www.politico.com/news/2020/03/06/joe-biden-bernie-brothers-twitter-123310.

13 Elliott, Tom. "Supercut! Trump Critics Would Never Use a Term Like 'Bloodbath'." Twitter, March 17, 2024. https://twitter.com/tomselliott/status/1769455728941547695.

14 Ries, Lora, and Simon Hankinson. "'Catch and Release' Has Become 'Greet and Release.'" The Heritage Foundation, June 15, 2023. https://www.heritage.org/immigration/commentary/catch-and-release-has-become-greet-and-release.

15 Spagat, Elliot. "Immigrants Waiting 10 Years in US Just to Get a Court Date." AP News, April 26, 2023. https://apnews.com/article/immigration-courts-wait-54bb5f7c18c4c37c6ca7f28231ff0edf.

16 Lindstrom, Rebecca, et al. "Did Laken Riley's Accused Killer Fall Through the Cracks of US Immigration Enforcement?" 11Alive, February 27, 2024. https://www.11alive.com/article/news/crime/jose-ibarra-accused-killer-laken-riley-georgia-immigration-system/85-0294133e-f5e1-4e2f-a2df-ab017b498508.

17 Doc Rudy, Soul Studios. "Ain't No Mountain High Enough (Extra HQ) - Marvin Gaye & Tammi Terrell." YouTube, August 4, 2011. https://www.youtube.com/watch?v=IC5PL0XImjw.

18 Har, Janie. "The Killing of a Nursing Student Out for a Run Highlights the Fears of Solo Female Athletes." AP News, February 24, 2024. https://apnews.com/article/runner-dead-university-georgia-women-safety-4b277117e82ab00d7e6c79672219a65f.

19 Daviscourt, Katie. "NY Post Headline Slammed for Saying Illegal Murder Suspect 'Panicked' When Laken Riley Fought Back." The Post Millennial,

February 28, 2024. https://thepostmillennial.com/ny-post-headline-slammed-for-saying-illegal-murder-suspect-panicked-when-laken-riley-fought-back.

[20] Donlevy, Katherine, and Yaron Steinbuch. "Nursing Student Laken Riley Tried to Call 911 Before Deadly Encounter with Migrant: Cops." New York Post, February 28, 2024. https://nypost.com/2024/02/28/us-news/laken-riley-likely-fought-her-murderer-profiler/.

[21] TOI Staff. "NY Times Admits Its Coverage of Gaza Hospital Blast Relied Too Heavily on Hamas Claims." Times of Israel, October 23, 2023. https://www.timesofisrael.com/ny-times-admits-its-coverage-of-gaza-hospital-blast-relied-too-heavily-on-hamas-claims/.

[22] "What to Know About the Gaza Strip and Who Controls It." Axios, October 21, 2023. https://www.axios.com/2023/10/21/gaza-strip-israel-hamas-war-demographics.

[23] *The New York Times*. "Editors' Note: Gaza Hospital Coverage." *The New York Times*, October 23, 2023. https://www.nytimes.com/2023/10/23/pageoneplus/editors-note-gaza-hospital-coverage.html.

[24] Yeung, Jessie, et al. "Hundreds Likely Dead in Gaza Hospital Blast, as Israeli Blockade Cripples Medical Response." CNN, October 24, 2023. https://edition.cnn.com/2023/10/17/middleeast/israel-gaza-rafah-crossing-week-2-tuesday-intl-hnk/index.html.

[25] McLaughlin, Charlotte. "BBC News Deputy CEO Admits 'Mistake' in Live Coverage of Gaza Hospital Bombing." *The Independent*, October 19, 2023. https://www.independent.co.uk/news/uk/bbc-news-bbc-gaza-grant-shapps-palestinian-b2432797.html.

[26] Ibid.

Chapter 19 — More Whistleblowers

Ah yes, the curious case of Uri Berliner.

On April 9, 2024, Berliner published an essay titled "I've Been at NPR for 25 Years. Here's How We Lost America's Trust," on The Free Press, a website owned by Bari Weiss, an independent journalist of the Twitter Files fame.[1]

In it, Berliner, senior business editor at NPR, effectively torpedoed his career with NPR by stating what public radio's detractors knew all along and what its supporters had possibly chosen to ignore — that over the past few years, the longtime leftist organization had sunk deeper, exhibiting what appeared to be cult-like behavior.[2]

Berliner wrote that NPR always leaned left but remained loyal to the teachings of true journalism.

"In recent years, however, that has changed," he wrote. "Today, those who listen to NPR or read its coverage online find something different: the distilled worldview of a very small segment of the U.S. population."[3]

With a zealot's blindness, NPR renounced the significance of the Laptop from Hell and the possibility of the COVID-19 virus emanating from a Wuhan lab leak, while elevating controversial U.S. Rep. Adam Schiff to deity status and allowing its own culture to be infested with the twisted ideology of DEI.[4]

"What's notable is the extent to which people at every level of NPR have comfortably coalesced around the progressive worldview," Berliner concluded. "And this, I believe, is the most damaging development at NPR: the absence of viewpoint diversity."5

Despite its dedication to DEI, Berliner noted the severe lack of political diversity, pointing out, "In D.C., where NPR is headquartered and many of us live, I found 87 registered Democrats working in editorial positions and zero Republicans. None."6

After reading Berliner's piece, I had to wonder what would drive a man whose entire essence was carved from left-leaning stone, as he describes it, to release such a controversial revelation to the public: "I'm Sarah Lawrence-educated, was raised by a lesbian peace activist mother, I drive a Subaru, and Spotify says my listening habits are most similar to people in Berkeley."7 Had he reached his threshold, his breaking point and was compelled to release his thoughts, or suffer the consequence of damaging his soul in perpetuity?

The day after Berliner's essay hit the internet, NPR responded, with Chief News Executive Edith Chapin disseminating a memo to staff, in which she defended the organization's practices and products. "We're proud to stand behind the exceptional work that our desks and shows do to cover a wide range of challenging stories," she wrote. "We believe that inclusion – among our staff, with our sourcing, and in our overall coverage – is critical to telling the nuanced stories of this country and our world."8

NPR's CEO, Katherine Maher, issued her own staff memo, where she framed Berliner's arguments and outlined NPR's place in society and its plans for the future. "NPR's service to this aspirational mission was called in question this week, in two distinct ways," she wrote. "The first was a critique of the quality of our editorial process and the integrity of our journalists. The second was a criticism of our people on the basis of who we are. Asking a question about whether we're living up to our mission should always be fair game: after all, journalism is nothing if not hard questions. Questioning whether our people are serving our mission with integrity, based on little more than the recognition of their identity, is profoundly disrespectful, hurtful, and demeaning."[9]

Despite NPR's protestations, Berliner's revelations triggered members of the media to dig into Maher's past social media posts. That garnered additional criticism "on everything from the First Amendment to misinformation to the idea that written history is tilted toward the worldview of white men," according to *The New York Post*.[10]

The next week, NPR suspended Berliner "for violating the network's policy against doing work outside the organization without first getting permission," according to *The New York Times*. A second violation would result in his termination, he was warned.[11]

And on April 17, NPR published a piece stating that Berliner had resigned and, in his letter, included a final shot at Maher. "I am resigning from NPR, a great American institution where I have worked for 25 years," Berliner wrote in an email to CEO Katherine Maher. "I respect the integrity of my colleagues and wish for NPR to thrive and do important journalism. But I cannot work in a newsroom where I am disparaged by a new CEO whose divisive views confirm the very problems at NPR I cite in my Free Press essay."[12]

Interestingly, NPR and Maher declined to comment on Berliner's resignation, according to... NPR.

We need more people like Uri Berliner, courageous men and women with integrity who are willing to step forward and call the industry out. Journalism, at one point, enjoyed a reputation as the source that cast a bright light on deceitful deeds done in the dark. Now it seems it must turn that light around on itself to correct its past sins. With the journalism industry rapidly evolving – with the rise of independent and citizen journalism – there are other opportunities to make money aside from the mainstream media. This, hopefully, will allow for more whistleblowers.

It's one thing for pundits on the outside to lay down a fusillade of condemnation on mainstream media, but to have it come from someone working in an influential position at one of the most prominent mainstream media outlets, such as Berliner, carries so much more weight.

For those of you out there considering similar actions, I support you.

---

[1] Berliner, Uri. « I've Been at NPR for 25 Years. Here's How We Lost America's Trust." thefp.com, April 9, 2024. https://www.thefp.com/p/npr-editor-how-npr-lost-americas-trust.

[2] Ibid.

[3] Ibid.

[4] Ibid.

[5] Ibid.

[6] Ibid.

[7] Ibid.

[8] Folkenflik, David. "NPR defends its journalism after senior editor says it has lost the public's trust." NPR, April 10, 2024. https://www.npr.org/2024/04/09/1243755769/npr-journalist-uri-berliner-trust-diversity.

[9] Maher, Katherine. "From NPR President and CEO Katherine Maher: Thoughts on our mission and our work." NPR, April 12, 2024. https://www.npr.org/sections/npr-extra/2024/04/12/1244456600/from-npr-president-and-ceo-katherine-maher-thoughts-on-our-mission-and-our-work.

[10] Steigrad, Alexandra. "NPR CEO slams Uri Berliner's 'bad faith distortion' of her woke social media posts." *The New York Post*, April 24, 2024. https://nypost.com/2024/04/24/media/nprs-katherine-maher-slams-uri-berliners-distortion-of-woke-social-media-posts/.

[11] Mullin, Banjamin. "NPR Suspends Editor Whose Essay Criticized the Broadcaster." *The New York Times*, April 16, 2024. https://www.nytimes.com/2024/04/16/business/media/npr-suspends-business-editor.html.

[12] Folkenflik, David. "NPR editor Uri Berliner resigns with blast at new CEO." NPR, April 17, 2024. https://www.npr.org/2024/04/17/1245283076/npr-editor-uri-berliner-resigns-ceo-katherine-maher.

Chapter 20 – Teach Journalism the Right Way

As outlined in Chapter 17, one of the main fronts of the battle for mainstream media to reclaim its position as a trusted source of news is by declaring a major shift to accurately and truthfully report the news. The other front is the isolated incubator world of higher education.

Over the past several decades, there has been, I believe, a concerted, systemic effort among American college and university journalism programs and professors to envenom the minds of impressionable young prospective journalists.

Students have been catechized into foot soldiers for political correctness. Instead of espousing critical thinking, journalism programs have outright eschewed it. Activism and advocacy are encouraged, when truly, journalism was never designed to be such a vehicle. The foundation of these false precepts is the belief that the readership is not intelligent enough to decide for themselves; instead, they must be told what to think.

The situation has now reached a point, as noted in Chapter 3, where the purveyors of this propaganda are infected with such a degree of hubris that they have become brazen in their declaration. All the easier to identify and refute them, I say.

In the spring of 2024, as college students adopted support for Hamas as the cause *du jour*, allegedly committing crimes such as vandalism, assault, and even kidnapping, some of their professors also joined in. In one image, Steven Thrasher, a professor of journalism at Northwestern University, wears a keffiyeh, a Palestinian scarf, while addressing students.

"To the Medill students and journalists within earshot, I say to you: Our work is not about objectivity," he said. "Our work is about you putting your brilliant minds to work and opening your compassionate hearts."[1]

Looking at Thrasher's bio on the Northwestern's Medill School of Journalism website, the professor's work is described as encouraging students "to draw upon history, theory, culture, and reporting to critically read and create media narratives."[2]

"Creating media narratives." What a shame that such a misguided belief was able to germinate and become acceptable in the once-hallowed halls of one of the top journalism schools in the country.

To pitch the battle against such deeply-institutionalized fallacies, there needs to be a hard-as-nails, fair crusader, someone of tremendous influence at the helm of a major university, who needs to take a hands-on approach, to rehabilitate its journalism program to return to focusing on free speech, critical thinking, fairness, and objectivity. This person's actions need to be done in the public eye with maximum exposure in the media. There will be formidable opposition, but that is where a steeled conviction will prove invaluable. Once the line is held, I believe there might be a domino effect that could take place among other colleges and universities.

---

[1] Glennon, Mark. "Death to Facts: Northwestern journalism prof Steven Thrasher tells pro-Palestinian demonstrators to reject objective reporting – Updated – Wirepoints." Wirepoints, April 30, 2024. https://wirepoints.org/death-to-facts-northwestern-journalism-prof-steven-thrasher-speaks-at-pro-palestinian-demonstration-rejecting-objective-reporting-wirepoints/.

[2] Steven Thrasher Assistant Professor and Daniel H. Renberg Chair https://www.medill.northwestern.edu/directory/faculty/steven-thrasher.html.

Chapter 21 – Resist Focusing on Race

In a 2005 interview on *60 Minutes*, actor Morgan Freeman told journalist Mike Wallace he finds the concept of Black History Month to be "ridiculous," because the implication is that the history of black Americans should only be restricted to one month.

"I don't want a Black History Month; black history is American history," Freeman said.

"But how are we going to get rid of racism…" Wallace asks.

"Stop talking about it. I'm going to stop calling you a white man and I'm going to ask you to stop calling me a black man. I know you as Mike Wallace, you know me as Morgan Freeman."[1]

But the problem is that many journalists are obsessed with talking about race and racism. There is more than one reason for this. One is because it stirs up visceral reactions from the American public, which translates into more readers and viewers, which means more money. Running a media company is a business, so I'm not denying the right to sell papers or ads on TV, but let's have some integrity and not go for the low-hanging fruit. Besides, it's been done so often the veil has been lifted; everyone sees what's going on in terms of race-baiting.

But beyond that, I submit they also inject race into their products as a virtue-signal for fear of being branded as racist if they do not. That's operating out of fear, something a journalist cannot do. This teaching is one manifestation of the woke ideology that has infected journalism.

Aside from someone being charged with a hate crime, or staging a race hoax, there is virtually no grounds to implant race into the equation in journalism; it serves only to generate friction between races. NDTV.com, a website out of New Delhi, India, has an aggregated section on their website titled "White police officer shoots black man."[2] In the section, you can peruse the latest headlines from the United States, where various news organizations have inseminated race into police-involved fatal shootings. But when was the last time you saw "Black cop shoots white man" or "Hispanic cop shoots Asian man"? You don't, though I feel pretty certain it happens. If we're truly going to focus on race, let's focus on all races, or else what can be concluded but that the media is focusing on white versus black for a disingenuous purpose?

A cop shooting a man could be a problem if the cop wasn't justified in doing so. But unless there is concrete evidence, or you have the *Minority Report* software – the Tom Cruise movie where cops can determine premeditation and motive for committing a crime – why would you assume race was a factor at all?

The media will tell you it's important to focus on white cops killing black men because there is an inordinate amount of these incidents happening around the country.

"Black men are 2.5 times more likely than white men to be killed by police in America, according to a 2019 study, which also predicted that 1 in 1,000 Black men would be killed by police over their lifetime," according to an article on the American Bar Association's website.[3] The article leads with the 2020 death of George Floyd in Minneapolis as he was being arrested by police.

But has the media ever considered that the reason black men are 2.5 times more likely than white men to be killed by police is that they are committing more violent crimes?

Floyd's death elicited a wide-ranging investigation by the U.S. Department of Justice, which, according to a *City Journal* story, "Though they constitute 18 percent of the city's population, blacks were responsible for 88 percent of Minneapolis homicides in which the race of the offender was known to the police. The rate of any violent crime among black Minneapolis residents is 27 times higher than among white residents."[4]

The cherry-on-top for the media is if a fatal shooting between a black man and police also appears at the outset to involve what some might consider excessive force.

In March 2024, some believe the media attempted to seize upon what may have appeared to be such an incident and possibly trigger another George Floyd-like riot-filled "Summer of Love." Dexter Reed died in a shootout with police in Chicago following a traffic stop. Many in the media zeroed in on how many shots were fired – 96 shots in 41 seconds – but failed to report that Reed shot at police first, that he refused to follow police's commands[5] and that police are trained to fire until a deadly threat is neutralized.[6] Reed should not have been carrying a gun, because he had been charged with felony gun possession,[7] but many news agencies omitted this or buried it in their stories. To top it off, at least two of the officers who responded to the incident were black, including the officer Reed wounded,[8] two facts that were conveniently left out of most reports.

In all incidents, but especially in delicate, tragic events, context matters. Some details trickle out in subsequent news stories, but typically, the initial story is most remembered, and, in many cases, readers don't get past the headline, according to copyblogger.com.[9]

Here is a sampling of headlines when the news of Reed's death broke, thanks to Straight Arrow News:[10]

The Washington Post: "Police fire 96 shots in 41 seconds, killing Black man during traffic stop."

Chicago Sun-Times: "Killing of Dexter Reed raises questions about Chicago police reform. 'The message is, go in guns blazing.'"

USA Today: "96 shots in 41 seconds: Seatbelt violation leads to death of Black Chicago motorist."

News organizations needed to ask themselves in Reed's case: "Do the races of anyone involved truly matter in this story?" and also, "On its surface, 96 shots really looks excessive, but let's wait and gather more information."

Journalists love talking about systemic racism, but they need to turn an introspective eye and realize these knee-jerk habits are in fact systemic practices that should be purged from the craft of journalism.

---

[1] *60 Minutes*. "Morgan Freeman on Black History Month." rickey2b4 YouTube channel. https://www.youtube.com/watch?v=GeixtYS-P3s.

[2] "White Police Officer Shoots Black Man." NDTV.com. https://www.ndtv.com/topic/white-police-officer-shoots-black-man.

[3] Shenkman, Drew, and Kelli Slade. "Police Reports Shouldn't Set the News Agenda: A Guide to Avoiding Systemic Racism in Reporting." American Bar Association, Jan. 22, 2021. https://www.americanbar.org/groups/communications_law/publications/communications_lawyer/fall2020/police-reports-shouldnt-set-news-agenda-guide-avoiding-systemic-racism-reporting/.

[4] Savolainen, Jukka, and John Paul Wright. "Maligning Minneapolis." *City Journal*, June 11, 2023. https://www.city-journal.org/article/biden-doj-claims-minneapolis-police-discriminate-but-ignores-crime-disparities#:~:text=Though%20they%20constitute%2018%20percent,was%20known%20to%20the%20police.

[5] Associated Press. "Chicago man opens fire on officers after failing to follow commands in deadly encounter." AP, April 10, 2024. https://www.foxnews.com/us/chicago-man-opens-fire-officers-failing-follow-commands-deadly-encounter.

[6] Lord, Debbie. « Here's why police don't shoot to wound in the case of deadly force." AJC.com, June 13, 2019. https://www.ajc.com/news/national/here-why-police-don-shoot-wound-the-case-deadly-force/IV4ohtIm6r8FaEMj78u1bO/.

[7] "Man killed during shootout with Chicago police was on pretrial release for a felony gun case, court records show." CWBchicago.com, March 23, 2024. https://cwbchicago.com/2024/03/man-killed-during-shootout-with-chicago-police-was-on-pretrial-release-for-a-felony-gun-case-court-records-show1.html.

[8] Parrella-Aureli, Ariel, et al. "Dexter Reed Shot Cop Before Officers Returned Fire 96 Times, Watchdog Says As Video Released (GRAPHIC VIDEO)." blockclubchicago.org, April 9, 2024. https://blockclubchicago.org/2024/04/09/police-shot-at-dexter-reed-96-times-in-41-seconds-during-deadly-shootout-watchdog-graphic-video/.

[9] "How to Write Magnetic Headlines." https://copyblogger.com/magnetic-headlines/#:~:text=On%20average%2C%208%20out%20of,get%20the%20next%20sentence%20read.

[10] Rucker, Karah, and Ian Kennedy. "Chicago cops who shot Dexter Reed say he fired first. How media told the story." Straight Arrow News, April 12, 2024. https://san.com/cc/chicago-cops-who-shot-dexter-reed-say-he-fired-first-how-media-told-the-story/.

Chapter 22 – No Donations

Accepting money from outside individuals, organizations, and groups as a media outlet is akin to making a deal with the devil. It sounds fantastic at the beginning, but at some point, ol' Lucifer comes to collect, and that ain't pretty.

Unfortunately, there appears to be a groundswell of support for this type of activity, largely a byproduct of the hard times media companies find themselves in. I would guess the thinking is, the money is going to help us continue to produce quality journalism, so does its source really matter?

Khadijah Costley White, assistant professor of journalism and media studies with the School of Communication and Information at Rutgers-New Brunswick, appeared to inadvertently present the conundrum of receiving outside funding, no matter the source. "In the UK you have the BBC, which is primarily government funded, so they have more freedom from advertisers," she said. "We have PBS and NPR, but they get very little public funding. They are very much beholden to the taste of their sponsors and audience, which is largely white and middle class." White advocates for increased government involvement, particularly the Federal Communications Commission. But the quandary is that no matter the source of the money, there is at least the appearance of that source extended influence over the coverage and content of the news, which harms a media outlet's credibility with the public.[1]

And the whole notion of NPR only receiving 1 percent from the government?[2] Throughout my journalism career, and probably long before that, the newsroom was a bustling marketplace of independent thought. And independent thought was the fiber, the soul, of what we did as journalists. It was why we held ourselves to such high standards. We couldn't be swayed, we couldn't be bought, we couldn't be influenced.

If there wasn't a physical wall between the newsroom and the advertising department, then there definitely was a figurative one. We didn't want any of those ad people thinking they could waltz over and purr at us to get a puff piece produced about one of their clients.

When I first heard of the concept of a cash infusion from the government, I was torn. On one hand, it sounded like job security, something we desperately needed, with all of the layoffs and newsroom-gutting that was going on. On the other hand, it felt like I had taken a dive into a vat of chicken fat. As a reporter, you have an organic distrust of the government. So let me get this straight, the federal government is lending a helping hand to newspapers because local news is vanishing? You expect me to believe that? Since when did any government – local, state, or federal – ever wish for more journalism?

If money is funneled to newspapers, are they then expected to cover the federal government as usual? So there would be no reprisals for going hard in the paint on the feds? How would our readership trust us if they ever caught wind of a government hand-out? And if we tried to hide the subsidies and the public eventually found out, well, a cover-up always makes things look worse.

The origins of the talk I heard in the newsroom back in the day referred to President Biden's $1.85 trillion social spending bill, which later gained the audacious name "Build Back Better."[3] It was eventually split into three separate bills,[4] but in all my searching, I could find no follow-up on whether or not the money made it into the coffers of newspapers.

I got that same greasy feeling when I read in May 2023 that Google inked a content distribution deal with *The New York Times*. Google, through its parent company, Alphabet, is the largest search engine on the internet and also owns another top search engine, YouTube.

"The deal includes the *Times*' participation in Google News Showcase, a product that pays publishers to feature their content on Google News and some other Google platforms, according to the report, which cited people familiar with the matter," according to a Reuters story, referencing a *Wall Street Journal* story, which broke the news. "The *Times* in February announced an expansion of its agreement with Google that included content distribution and subscriptions."[5]

So you've got a Cthulhu-level online force in Google now with its claws sunk into one of the most well-known and well-respected media outlets. A story by The Verge says there are upwards of 450 news sites that are on the Google payroll. Talk about narrative control. Now you have 450 news outlets who more than likely won't print or produce one negative thing about Google or any of its assets. It's actually an ingenious move on Google's part, and even if those news outlets were to exercise true journalism, the appearance of impropriety still hangs over everything.[6]

With it being so tough for the media industry right now, I know it's hard not to turn down some serious green, but this is not the way; which begs the question, what is the way? As tough but also simple as it sounds, media outlets have to make money on their own. Strange concept, I know, but in this way, they mitigate any appearance of impropriety and conflict-of-interest.

Bollinger the Big Donation Booster

Lee Bollinger served as president of Columbia University for more than 20 years, ending his tenure in June 2023. That's very impressive, so props to him for that. It seems that Bollinger, whose background includes work as a lawyer, professor, and administrator,[7] shares my overall passion for journalism, but sadly, that is where the similarities between us end. In 2010, he published a book titled *Uninhibited, Robust, and Wide-Open: A Free Press for a New Century* in which one of his proposals is that the government should fund the media. To ensure I understood Bollinger's points completely, I bought his book off Amazon.com for $1.25 and to my absolute delight, once I received it, I found he had autographed the book for its previous owner!

In this book, Bollinger talks about the rise of the internet and how it has facilitated a global connectivity not previously imagined. "The world is becoming more integrated, moving inexorably (or so it would seem) toward becoming a single society," he writes.[8]

That depends on how you look at it. Some would say the globalist movement is inevitable and beneficial, while others would say it's fine for nations to interact, but that retaining their autonomy is paramount. He also mentions the U.S. investing in countries around the world and "emerging markets," other countries becoming power players. The result, he asserts, is an interdependency.[9]

> "Given the rapid changes in the world due to globalization, where we have far less understanding than we need, and given the insufficiency of both political and academic institutions to deal well with what is happening, the press and journalism should take

on a greater-than-usual role in helping us to figure out what issues we need to address."[10]

Similar to some of the purveyors of fraudulent journalism, I think he's got it wrong here. Journalism isn't about shaping or guiding policies, or even, at the far end, pushing an ideology; journalism *reflects* what is going on in the world, it *informs*. It lays it all out there for people, and then allows them to make informed decisions. It provides a snapshot, a truncated version, and people can take that and do their own research from there. It provides the spark for further digging and delving.

Let's look at another passage.

"Americans want and need the nation's press to be engaged journalistically with the wider world." *Do they, though?* I'm not so sure they really do. Most Americans care about America first. It's like when you're on an airplane and they say, put your own mask on first and then help the person next to you. The lesson is you're not going to be able to help others to the fullest extent without first operating at your optimum level.[11]

Here's another misguided statement: The loss of revenue, brought on by the internet, "May become so grave as to require injections of public funds; indeed, my own view is that this will prove to be the only way to sustain a free press over time."[12]

Wrong. Replace "free" with "bought" when referring to the press. It's possible that in 2010 Bollinger never envisioned what the internet could become, the ingenuity of independent journalists having the courage to report stories the mainstream media won't.

Bollinger posits that a media source can only check and monitor the government if you are a big company with lots of resources. "The press cannot be composed of a multitude of isolated individuals or small organizations, however much each may be committed to high-quality journalism."[13]

Wrong again, how do you think journalism started? It started small, just one dude and his press. That's the backbone of journalism. And now, with the internet, that's exactly what we're getting via independent and citizen journalism. It's an equal playing field. The public reaps the benefits, because they can look at multiple sources – here's what this big outlet is saying about this incident, but then over here, I found someone posted video from the event and it tells a slightly, or maybe drastically, different story.

Whether by coordination or coincidence, in the winter 2009-10 edition of *Columbia Magazine*, David J. Craig wrote a piece titled "J-school Report: Local News Needs Handout," in which he talks about a report, "The Reconstruction of American Journalism," written by Leonard Downie, Jr., a former executive editor of *The Washington Post* and a professor at Arizona State University, and Michael Schudson, a historian of journalism and a Columbia J-school professor.[14]

"Downie and Schudson insist that the American marketplace no longer can sustain a vital free press," Craig wrote. "They say government intervention is needed especially to prop up local news operations, as local coverage has been hurt the most by newspaper cutbacks and shutdown."[15]

More than a decade later, Columbia was still beating the drum about government handouts in an article written by Robert W. McChesney and John Nichols, titled "The Local Journalism Initiative: a proposal to protect and extend democracy."[16]

"We need the funding to support independent, competitive, professional local news media," McChesney and Nichols write. "That money must come from the government. It is the only viable option at a point when the market has shown that it cannot begin to sustain existing media, let alone usher in a renewal of bold speak-truth-to-power journalism."[17]

I suppose 2010's "Reconstruction" didn't gain a foothold in Washington, so like pouring perfume on a pig, they re-packaged and re-launched it and called it an "Initiative," still bemoaning how the market, loss of advertising, the internet, and cutbacks have decimated local journalism and how the only hope is for government to come galloping in on a shining steed, blasting money out of handheld cannons.

There's just something wrong on a visceral level with taking money from an outside source. When I worked as a reporter, we couldn't accept anything from sources, not even a drink or a sandwich.

You can try to justify it all you want, but in the end, it goes against everything that journalism was founded on – a *free* press. You can't be free if you are beholden to an entity, organization, or agency. And sure, the government can say there's "no strings attached," but we know how power corrupts, despite the best of intentions. You can just imagine that through back channels a politician might communicate a "strong suggestion" to a media outlet that receives funding to either kill or push a certain story. To drive the point home, the politician might issue a thinly-veiled threat to pull funding for the news source.

Bollinger insists, "there have been strikingly few instances of government abuse," in public and private research universities. That's a pretty naive statement to make; there shouldn't be *any*. It's like saying, "Well, there's only been a few instances where a killer whale in captivity has attacked someone, so I guess that's okay."[18]

Not only that, but this belief is in direct opposition with the Society of Professional Journalists' ethical code, which states, "Avoid conflicts of interest, real or perceived. Disclose unavoidable conflicts."[19]

A news source is nothing without its credibility — its ability to be believed — and credibility is hamstrung by conflicts of interest.

The SPJ ethical code also lists a link to a column by Tony Rogers on thoughtco.com:

> "Don't Accept Freebies or Gifts From Sources. People will often try to curry favor with reporters by offering them gifts of various sorts. But taking such freebies opens the reporter up to the charge that he can be bought."[20]

Here is what the First Amendment, as part of the Bill of Rights, which was ratified on Dec. 15, 1791, states, according to congress.gov:[21]

> "Congress shall make no law respecting an establishment of religion, or prohibiting the free exercise thereof; or abridging the freedom of speech, or of the press; or the right of the people peaceably to assemble, and to petition the Government for a redress of grievances."[22]

Prior to Dec. 15, 1791, when the Bill of Rights was ratified, as states and commonwealths were breaking free of England's iron grip, the press played an integral role. Those who sought independence printed in the darkness to expose the tyranny to the light. And what did England want so desperately to confiscate to control the people? Well, the presses, of course.

In 2020, David Wilson published a piece titled "Freedom of the Press in the eyes of the Founding Fathers."[23]

"From the evidence that we have, it appears that our founding fathers understood the power of the press and its need to remain free of government control, for communication with their State and for greater communication amongst the new

Nation," Wilson wrote. "As the Virginia Declaration of Rights put it 'That the freedom of the press is one of the greatest bulwarks of liberty and can never be restrained but by despotic governments.'"[24]

In the article, Wilson also lists several entries of states' Bills of Rights or Constitutions where they mention freedom of the press, all prior to 1791. Several say that such a liberty must be "inviolably" preserved. I had to look that one up; according to Oxford Languages it means "never to be broken, infringed, or dishonored." Now that's some powerful stuff.[25]

One interesting nugget from Bollinger's book is the mention of a federal agency known as the Office of Strategic Influence, which was formed in 2002 during the war on terror. The office was tasked with essentially creating and proliferating propaganda to gain sympathizers in adversarial countries.[26]

"These efforts would include the deliberate use of misinformation when it was deemed appropriate," Bollinger wrote. Did you catch that word, *misinformation,* used by the U.S. government more than two decades ago? So, the government's intent then was to weaponize words, but for a noble cause. However, in a subsequent administration, the same word was used to describe content that ran contrary to its agenda.[27]

In February 2022, The Associated Press announced that the reception of "philanthropic grants" would enable the global news agency to deploy more than two dozen reporters to cover "climate issues" around the world.[28]

"The AP's new team, with journalists based in Africa, Brazil, India, and the United States, will focus on climate change's impact on agriculture, migration, urban planning, the economy, culture and other areas," reporter David Bauder wrote.[29]

Sounds very altruistic. And $8 million over three years is a nice chunk of change. The grant comes from several wealthy donors, most of which, I'd be willing to bet, have private jets. How does that help the environment? Also, all of those organizations support radical climate change plans, despite that there are many professional opinions to the contrary. It begs the question of whether the AP could write a story challenging the climate change doctrine or even provide both sides of the argument.

In fact, the article goes on to say that about 50 AP journalists' jobs are funded by grants.

"AP accepts money to cover certain areas but without strings attached; the funders have no influence on the stories that are done," according to AP news vice president Brian Carovillano.[30]

But then the article says: "For Carovillano, it was getting used to the idea that funders weren't just being generous; they had their own goals to achieve. 'This is a mutually beneficial arrangement,' he said."[31]

And what, pray tell, would those "goals" of the funders be?

---

[1] Intrabartola, Lisa. "How Trump Shaped the Media." Rutgers University, January 19, 2021. https://www.rutgers.edu/news/how-trump-shaped-media.

[2] Husock, Howard. "The Truth about NPR's Funding - and Its Possible Future." The Hill, April 17, 2023. https://thehill.com/opinion/campaign/3950550-the-truth-about-nprs-funding-and-its-possible-future/.

[3] Tracy, Marc. "Local News Outlets Could Reap $1.7 Billion in Build Back Better Aid." *New York Times*, Nov. 28, 2021. https://www.nytimes.com/2021/11/28/business/media/build-back-better-local-news.html.

[4] Build Back Better Plan. https://en.wikipedia.org/wiki/Build_Back_Better_Plan

[5] "New York Times to Get Around $100 Million from Google over Three Years." Reuters, May 8, 2023. https://www.reuters.com/business/media-telecom/new-york-times-get-around-100-million-google-over-three-years-wsj-2023-05-08/.

6 Porter, Jon. "Google Now Pays 450 Sites to Bring You Free News, Including Some Paywalled Stories." The Verge, February 10, 2021. https://www.theverge.com/2021/2/10/22276544/google-news-showcase-uk-argentina-launch-license-paywall-content.

7 "Lee Bollinger." Wikipedia, March 30, 2024. https://en.wikipedia.org/wiki/Lee_Bollinger.

8 Bollinger, Lee C. *Uninhibited, Robust, and Wide-Open: A Free Press for a New Century*. Oxford University Press, 2010.

9 Ibid.

10 Ibid.

11 Ibid.

12 Ibid.

13 Ibid.

14 Craig, David J. "J-School Report: Local News Needs Handout." *Columbia Magazine*, Winter 2009-2010. https://magazine.columbia.edu/article/j-school-report-local-news-needs-handout.

15 Ibid.

16 McChesney, Robert W., and John Nichols. "The Local Journalism Initiative: A Proposal to Protect and Extend Democracy." *Columbia Journalism Review*, November 30, 2021. https://www.cjr.org/business_of_news/the-local-journalism-initiative.php.

17 Ibid.

18 Bollinger, Lee C. "Journalism Needs Government Help." *The Wall Street Journal*, July 14, 2010. https://www.wsj.com/articles/SB10001424052748704629804575324782605510168.

19 "SPJ Code of Ethics." Society of Professional Journalists, September 6, 2014. https://www.spj.org/ethicscode.asp.

20 Rogers, Tony. "6 Ways Reporters Can Avoid Conflicts of Interest." ThoughtCo, February 13, 2019. https://www.thoughtco.com/avoid-conflicts-of-interest-2073885.

21 U.S. Constitution - First Amendment. Accessed March 31, 2024. https://constitution.congress.gov/constitution/amendment-1/.

22 Ibid.

23 Wilson, David. "Freedom of the Press in the Eyes of the Founding Fathers." Colonial Williamsburg, July 7, 2020.

https://www.colonialwilliamsburg.org/learn/living-history/freedom-press-eyes-founding-fathers/.

[24] Ibid.

[25] Ibid.

[26] Bollinger, Lee C. *Uninhibited, Robust, and Wide-Open: A Free Press for a New Century*. Oxford University Press, 2010.

[27] Ibid.

[28] Bauder, David. "Climate Grant Illustrates Growth in Philanthropy-Funded News." AP News, February 16, 2022. https://apnews.com/article/science-business-arts-and-entertainment-journalism-united-states-087d1d5dd7189c529fe5d7a21a1ffb5f.

[29] Ibid.

[30] Ibid.

[31] Ibid.

Chapter 23 – Continue Covering Local News

In 2023, the Medill School of Journalism produced a massive report, "The State of Local News," complete with pie charts, graphs, a triangular hierarchy, and maps.

> "In recent years, hundreds of scholars – in the U.S. and around the globe – have begun to train their critical lens on both the issues and solutions confronting local news organizations. These include economists, political scientists, sociologists and historians, as well as communication researchers. They are collecting and analyzing data, both to map and to identify communities at risk, as well as to study the impact of losing local news on communities without it."[1]

There's no need to throw all sorts of scholars at this and expend money and hours of research. Let me sum it up. Newspapers abandoned local news because they didn't think it was making them money. But in doing so, they lost readers, and subsequently, even more money, because local news is what matters to local residents. It helps them stay connected to their community.

I watched this happen over the course of two decades in my journalism career. The newspapers in York – I worked for one from 1999-2004 and the other from 2004-2021 – each had a cadre of "stringers" or freelance writers, who would cover local news and get paid by the article. They primarily covered local news, including municipal government meetings and human-interest stories, essentially the lower-level stories that full-time reporters were too busy to cover. But slowly, over time, their numbers began to dwindle, as more than likely ownership considered getting rid of them as a quick fix to save money. What they may not have realized is that local news is actually the backbone, the bread-and-butter of small papers. Think about it – why else would you buy a hometown paper? You want to know what's happening in your backyard because that's news you can't get anywhere else. If you want to know what's happening in the nation or the world, there are plenty of places for that. So it became a Catch-22: the newspaper is hemorrhaging money, so you cut your stringer budget, but then because you stopped covering local news, you lost even more money.

As discussed in Chapter 15, there currently is a return to local news sweeping the country, and it's being driven by true local ownership, not chains. But newspaper chains can get in on the action if they want. They can re-dedicate staff to covering local government and education meetings, to get their finger back on the pulse of the community. They could take it one step further and do a front-page story stating publicly their re-dedication and asking for the public's support and suggestions.

Here's another outlet that I discovered is flying the local news banner high. In 2023, the LNP Media Group in Lancaster, Pennsylvania, which operated one of the biggest, most successful newspapers in the Keystone State, became a subsidiary of WITF, a public radio station in Harrisburg, Pennsylvania.[2]

Following the announcement of the collaboration, WITF made it clear that the group would focus on local news, stating they would "collaboratively expand and diversify local news media platforms, educational programs and forums for civic engagement" and "build on local journalism that shines a light on government decision-making, serves as a check on public spending and holds elected leaders accountable."[3]

In a way, it's unfortunate that a news source would have to spell out, to the public no less, that they will focus on local news, when that used to be a given. It's also refreshing because as I have said, I believe that is a key to success, but also now that it's out there, people will hold them to it.

But, to be fair, WITF's radio station is an NPR affiliate, while its TV station of the same call letters falls under the PBS banner. So, although they appear to be doing an admirable job covering local news, they still operate under the specter of a media source receiving government funding.

---

[1] Abernathy, Penelope Muse. "The State of Local News." Local News Initiative, November 16, 2023.
https://localnewsinitiative.northwestern.edu/projects/state-of-local-news/2023/report/#possibilities.

[2] Brod, Robby. "What you need to know about WITF's new partnership with LNP | LancasterOnline." WITF, April 28, 2023.
https://www.witf.org/2023/04/28/what-you-need-to-know-about-witfs-new-partnership-with-lnp-lancasteronline/.

[3] WITF. "A Leap Forward for Local Journalism, Community Education and Civic Engagement in Central Pennsylvania."
https://www.witf.org/about/witflnp/.

Chapter 24 – Cover Crime the Way It Should Be Covered

Over the past several years, we've seen a massive shift in the way crime is covered by the media. Suspects are treated in a kinder, gentler manner, mugshots are not used, and many everyday crimes that impact citizens are ignored. Apparently, you can't even call it the "crime beat" anymore – it's "public safety," or some other vanilla derivative. We've been told this change was the right thing to do, that it is a far more equitable manner of producing crime content. Well, I'm here to tell you the experiment failed. The reason crime was covered a certain way for centuries was because it worked. It was comprehensive, balanced, and courageous.

But now we've reached a point where those who cover crime the way it should be are vilified. In 2023, a longtime Philadelphia-based TV crime reporter, Steve Keeley, faced criticism from several local pundits who said his coverage makes them "cringe," and is "disturbing" and "harmful," according to *The Washington Times*.[1]

The flashpoint for the condemnation appears to be two columns written in as many days by Victor Fiorillo of *Philadelphia Magazine*, in which he cites a study[2] that determined Keeley's employer, Fox 29, had the highest percentage of articles on its website that dealt with crime and safety. (It's interesting to note Fiorillo leaves out the word "safety" when he mentions this statistic.)[3]

From Fiorillo's columns, it's clear he is fixated on such superficial factors such as Keeley's looks and delivery, saying the reporter is "tan," "buffish," and "animated." Fiorillo seems to be proud that he named Keeley the "Worst Reporter to Follow If You Need an Occasional Dose of Good News." Well, do tell, who is the best reporter in Philly if you want the highest dose of rainbows and unicorns?4

Another of Fiorillo's columns then amplifies the voices that he sparked from his first: NPR-affiliate WHYY's Cherri Gregg. "Steve Keeley FOX 29's coverage of crime – definitely makes me cringe. Crime coverage can be very harmful and scares people," Fiorillo quotes Gregg writing on Facebook. *Philadelphia Inquirer* columnist Jenice Armstrong was up next, with Fiorillo quoting a post from Armstrong on Facebook, which states, "His (Keeley's) Twitter feed is also disturbing." On the contrary, it's the cold, hard reality of what's going on in the city. It's necessary, because most people want the truth, they want transparency and want to be informed, warts and all. Better to know the bad news is happening rather than pretending it doesn't and then getting blindsided by it.5

Every news outlet needs to have a Steve Keeley. He should not be an outlier, a pariah; he should be a necessary element of a media organization's extensive crime coverage. Sadly, this view is counter to a movement spearheaded by journalism think-tanks to overhaul how crime is covered. My jump down the rabbit-hole began with a May 16, 2023 tweet by Richard Hanania: "Effort under way to change crime coverage at the local level to be more "responsible" and "ethical." This involves, you guessed it, shaping the coverage to not reflect statistical realities regarding who commits crime."6

I did some digging and determined one of the sources of this new wave of crime coverage was the Poynter Institute, a Florida-based professional journalism education organization. A May 15, 2023 story by Barbara Allen on the institute's website provides details about an initiative known as "Transforming Crime Reporting into Public Safety Journalism."[7]

From what I can tell, the premise is that there is something systemically wrong with the way crime was covered by the media, and so it was somehow decided that an industry-sweeping re-education of sorts was necessary. You can see this indoctrination begins with the name. They're strongly suggesting that newsrooms no longer refer to it as crime coverage or police reporting, but public safety. But that's only the name; it appears it goes far deeper than that. This movement seems to have gained popularity. There were 44 newsrooms that underwent the training in 2022 and nearly 30 in 2023, according to the story.[8]

"Over the course of seven months, instructors and coaches will introduce a series of change management tools that will guide newsrooms as they transform their coverage, step by step," the story states.[9]

Step-by-step. So it's a cookie-cutter way of doing things? Their way or the highway? The Poynter Institute appears to kick things up a notch, sounding eerily reminiscent of William H. White's concept of "groupthink."

American psychologist Janis Irving described groupthink as "The more amiability and esprit de corps there is among the members of a policy-making-in-group, the greater the danger that independent critical thinking will be replaced by groupthink, which is likely to result in irrational and dehumanizing actions directed against out-groups."[10]

I wonder how the Poynter instructors would react if someone challenged them on any of their teachings. It doesn't sound like there would be any room for critical thinking in the curriculum, and critical thinking is imperative when you're a journalist and also a consumer of media content.

Poynter talks about best practices for covering incidents such as sexual assault and suicide. I can tell you that in the newsroom at which I worked, there were already protocols in place. Yes, we covered sexual assaults, but never revealed a victim's name or any other identifying information, unless they came forward on their own. In one instance, I interviewed Danielle Keener, a sexual assault survivor, because she and her counselor had approached me and said she wanted to go public as part of her healing. Another example would be a woman who was raped on the Rail Trail in York City. She revealed herself on Facebook in an effort to catch the perpetrator. Despite making several posts in a very public forum, I reached out to her and asked permission to use what she had written, plus used some additional quotes from her.

And as far as suicides, our policy was that unless it was in a public place that drew widespread interest and affected others – say in the middle of a mall or on a busy highway – we didn't cover it.

One of Poynter's lead instructors, Kelly McBride, brings up the industry phrase "If it bleeds, it leads," as if it's archaic and barbaric. When you take the time to examine the phrase, there is a nuanced meaning within. First, it's a matter of giving the people what they clamor for; stories about tragedies are popular, hence the leading part. It's human nature to read about tragedy because it makes one feel better. "Well, glad that wasn't me," they might think. But also, there is a survival element to it as well. It's important to know what's going on in the environment around you to stay alive. It's called "situational awareness." Beyond that, it bears repeating that journalism is a public service, but also a business, so you're going to want to cover things that people want to read, because otherwise, you'll go out of business.

"Most of the reporters and editors I encounter really want to do better work," McBride said. "But newsroom systems and culture make it hard to change."[11]

During my journalism career, I took it upon myself to gain a better understanding of traumatic situations and how they affect people, eventually being named an Ochberg Fellow with the Dart Center for Journalism and Trauma. I had an amazing experience in New Orleans at the Dart Center symposium in 2004, meeting other crime reporters and war correspondents. Our cohort included a woman who took pictures of the Killing Fields in Cambodia, a man who had written a story about a sexual assault victim who had tracked down his perpetrator and exacted brutal retribution with an ax, and a photographer who had suffered PTSD from covering the Sept. 11 terrorist attacks in New York City.

Whether through Poynter or not, I saw firsthand "change" in crime coverage at my paper before I left in 2021, when I was told to stop covering daily violent crime and focus on issue-oriented pieces. Here's a solution: Why not have both? We can have the in-depth pieces that examine the underlying or overarching societal issues and also have the day-to-day crime coverage. That way, when you research and write your bigger pieces, you can reference the smaller stories, which provide the foundation.

Oh and no mugshots, I was told, because it was unfair to minorities, even though whites were also committing crimes and getting arrested. The only exception to use a mugshot was for an individual who was currently wanted and considered armed-and-dangerous.

So there's the idea of re-engineering the crime beat, and also the concept of defunding it altogether. I stumbled upon this wonderful piece from 2021 called, you guessed it, "Defund the crime beat."[12]

"It's racist, classist, fear-based clickbait masking as journalism," Chappell and Rispoli write. "It creates lasting harm for the communities that newsrooms are supposed to serve. And because it so rarely meets the public's needs, it's almost never newsworthy, despite what Grizzled Gary in his coffee-stained shirt says from his perch at the copy desk," the screed by Tauhid Chappell and Mike Rispoli reads. "This should be the year where we finally abolish the crime beat. Study after study shows how the media's overemphasis on crime makes people feel less safe than they really are and negatively shapes public policy around the criminal–legal system. And study after study shows that it's racist and inhumane."[13]

"Grizzled Gary?" I guess that's me.

Wrong on all counts. Covering crime is as un-racist as you can get. As a reporter, you catch wind of a crime, either from the scanner, a police news release, social media, or another source. Then you track down the charging documents, which are sworn legal documents signed by a judge. You call police for clarification. You track down the victims or their families. You talk to neighbors to see what their reaction is or if they witnessed anything. Maybe the mayor makes a statement. It doesn't start with someone's ethnicity or race. Who commits the crime is not part of the equation; it is the crime itself and how it affects the community.

I disagree that it causes people to feel less safe. What are we to do, sequester them? Pretend crime doesn't exist? An informed community is a better-prepared community. I can't even begin to tell you how many people have told me they appreciated what I did for 20-plus years.

Then there's this part I love: "There's a desperate need to attract as many eyeballs as possible to make a buck," as if making money is evil. Again, people forget journalism is a service to the public, but it's also a business. *The news doesn't report itself.* You need to pay people to do it and that takes money.[14]

Remember all those efforts to "defund the police" in 2020? What happened in their wake? Crime ran rampant and city councils pulled a 180 and re-funded the police because they realized what a moronic move that was. Ever read Dave Grossman's "On Sheep, Wolves, and Sheepdogs"? If you don't have the sheepdogs (police), there is a direct path between the wolves (criminals) and the sheep (people like Chappell and Rispoli). The problem is that even though the sheep need the sheepdogs, they begin to resent them and might even begin to have misgivings about allowing them to defend other sheep.[15]

Or how about Oregon making hard drugs like fentanyl and heroin legal? Yeah, that worked out well.[16] Four years later, drug possession was recriminalized.[17]

In this case, news outlets modifying or dropping crime coverage won't have such a drastic result on society, but I believe it will affect their bottom line. If you don't provide citizens the crime coverage it wants and needs, they will find it elsewhere and your newsrooms will suffer, as we have seen.[18]

Mugshots, should, without a doubt, be used in the media. The American people have a right to see the face of an individual who has been charged with a crime. To make a concerted effort to conceal an accused's identity creates the impression that the media is protecting someone who allegedly committed a crime. In many states, mugshots are a matter of public record, so therefore, they should be available to the public. The media exists to do things other people can do, but don't have the time or energy to do so. In many states, a mugshot is public record, as is an affidavit of probable cause, but are people lining up at the appropriate offices to get these things? No, they aren't; because even though they have the capacity, they are busy living their own lives. So they pay a little bit of money so a reporter can do it for them. The great thing is that anyone can decide not to view a mugshot if they do not wish to. There is also the notion of personifying evil. You want to see the face of the individual who allegedly gunned down the 10-year-old girl on the street. Some people wish to look into the face of evil as a means of conquering it.

As I said before, the bread-and-butter of local news is about covering town council and school board meetings; and I would argue that equally as important is crime coverage, done the right way.

---

[1] Murtaugh, Tim. "In Crime-Ridden Philly, Liberals Blast Journalist Steve Keeley for Reporting What's Happening." *The Washington Times*, March 16, 2023. https://www.washingtontimes.com/news/2023/mar/16/in-crime-ridden-philly-liberals-blast-journalist-s/.

[2] Stroud, Natalie Jomini, et al. "The News Philadelphians Use: Analyzing the Local Media Landscape." Center for Media Engagement, February 27, 2023. https://mediaengagement.org/research/the-news-philadelphians-use/.

[3] Fiorillo, Victor. "'If It Bleeds, It Leads' Is Alive and Well at Fox29." *Philadelphia Magazine*, March 9, 2023. https://www.phillymag.com/news/2023/03/09/fox-29-steve-keeley-philadelphia-crime/.

[4] Ibid.

[5] Fiorillo, Victor. "Fox 29's Steve Keeley Under Fire from Reporters and Councilperson for Crime Coverage." *Philadelphia Magazine*, March 10, 2023. https://www.phillymag.com/news/2023/03/10/steve-keeley-fox-29/.

[6] Hanania, Richard. "Effort Under Way to Change Crime Coverage at the Local Level to Be More 'Responsible' and 'Ethical.' This Involves, You Guessed It, Shaping the Coverage to Not Reflect Statistical Realities Regarding Who Commits Crime." Twitter, May 16, 2023. https://twitter.com/RichardHanania/status/1658509916909477890.

[7] Allen, Barbara. "Poynter Announces the 27 Newsrooms Accepted into Transforming Crime Reporting into Public Safety Journalism." Poynter, May 15, 2023. https://www.poynter.org/from-the-institute/2023/poynter-announces-the-28-newsrooms-accepted-into-transforming-crime-reporting-into-public-safety-journalism/.

8 Ibid.

9 Ibid.

10 Looti, Mohammad. "Groupthink in Psychology." Psychological Scales, November 19, 2022. https://scales.arabpsychology.com/2022/11/19/groupthink-2/.

11 Allen, Barbara. "Poynter Announces the 27 Newsrooms Accepted into Transforming Crime Reporting into Public Safety Journalism." Poynter, May 15, 2023. https://www.poynter.org/from-the-institute/2023/poynter-announces-the-28-newsrooms-accepted-into-transforming-crime-reporting-into-public-safety-journalism/.

12 Chappell, Tauhid, and Mike Rispoli. "Defund the Crime Beat." NiemanLab, accessed March 31, 2024. https://www.niemanlab.org/2020/12/defund-the-crime-beat/.

13 Ibid.

14 Ibid.

15 LTC (Ret) Grossman, Dave. "On Sheep, Wolves, and Sheepdogs." mwkworks, accessed March 31, 2024. https://www.mwkworks.com/onsheepwolvesandsheepdogs.html.

16 Abizaid, Dana. "'It Has Been Pretty Awful': First State to Decriminalize Hard Drugs Looking to Reverse Liberal Experiment." The Daily Caller, November 19, 2023. https://dailycaller.com/2023/11/19/first-state-decriminalize-hard-drugs-reverse-liberal-experiment/.

17 Campbell, Josh, Shelton, Shania and Iger, Kaanita. "Oregon governor to sign bill re-criminalizing possession of certain drugs into law." CNN, March 8, 2024. https://www.cnn.com/2024/03/08/politics/oregon-drug-laws-recriminalization/index.html

18 Post Editorial Board. "Liberal Media Say We Should Stop Covering Crime, Because It's Hurting Dems." *The New York Post*, November 30, 2022. https://nypost.com/2022/11/30/liberal-media-say-we-should-stop-covering-crime-because-its-hurting-dems/.

Chapter 25 – Have Business People Run the Business of Newspapers

How about installing actual business people to run the business of newspapers? It's something I considered while I was still a reporter. I noticed that many of those at the top of the corporate ladder making major business decisions were people who had started as editors or reporters and worked their way up to positions of power.

To me, that doesn't make any sense. As "Rowdy" Roddy Piper once said, it's "like bringing a knife to a gunfight." Why would you want someone whose mind is attuned to creativity, to generating content, to then be making complex business decisions that affect the company's survival? No, you want someone who has been in the trenches and cut their teeth in the business world! Then they can easily apply that experience, those principles, to the business of newspapers.

I've seen it happen in my career. You have an ambitious reporter or editor who rises up through the ranks over the years until they find themselves in an administrative position. It's possible that prior to that, they may have been concerned about the craft of journalism, so now, balancing that with taking steps to ensure the sustainability of the news organization may prove to be an insurmountable prospect. It's a classic example of the Peter Principle, where one is continuously promoted until they reach a level of incompetence.[1]

In the previous chapter, I mentioned the concerted effort to eliminate mugshots from use in the media. If I were to venture a guess, I would suspect that whoever developed that idea was a reporter or editor, not a true businessperson, because they would have realized what a monetization bonanza mugshots could be if managed correctly.

---

[1] Hayes, Adam. "The Peter Principle: What It Is and How to Overcome It." Inventopedia.com, Feb. 25, 2024.
https://www.investopedia.com/terms/p/peter-principle.asp#:~:text=%25%2025%25%200%25-,What%20Is%20the%20Peter%20Principle%3F,a%20level%20of%20respective%20incompetence.

Chapter 26 – Get Rid of Personality-driven News

If I was tasked with engineering a comeback for a cable news channel, the first order of business would be to abolish what I call *personality-driven news*. It seems that many of the main cable news outlets design their programming around personalities. I suspect the idea is that the news itself isn't exciting enough, you have to have an engaging, wise-cracking or otherwise charismatic anchor to constrict the show around.

A lot of the big names have their own show, typically based on a tacky play-on-words with their name: *The ReidOut* with Joy Reid, Erin Burnett *OutFront*, *The Ingraham Angle* with Laura Ingraham, and Anderson Cooper's *Anderson Cooper 360*.

And these guys and gals are making millions. Heck, if I could find someone willing to pay me $20 million a year (Cooper's salary), I would be a happy man indeed. Who am I to disparage what salary a person is able to negotiate?

A February 2024 story for InTouch indicated CNN's new CEO Mark Thompson, in hopes of leveling out a ratings freefall, was considering dismissing some of the network's heavyweights – who all have their own shows – including Cooper, Chris Wallace, Wolf Blitzer, and Jake Tapper.[1]

"Anderson knows he's on the chopping block because he makes a whopping $20 million a year. He's already started looking for a new gig!" a network insider exclusively told InTouch. "Chris Wallace takes $8 million and figures he's a likely target, too!"[2]

"Sources say he [Thompson] has no use for the star system and the hefty salaries that come with it," according to the InTouch article. "He's reportedly seeking to replace marquee names with talent who built their audiences on social media – including former FOX and NBC anchor Megyn Kelly, who has 1.72 million subscribers on YouTube."[3]

Although, based on the Reuters study, maybe media companies should hire influencers to read the news on various social media platforms, according to a story on FOXnews.com.[4]

"A study conducted for the Reuters Institute for the Study of Journalism, part of Britain's University of Oxford, found 55% of TikTok users and 52% of Instagram users get their news from 'personalities' on the respective platforms," the story states. "The figure of those who get their news from mainstream media and journalists on those same platforms falls to just 33% on TikTok and 42% on Instagram, per the 2023 Digital News Report."[5]

The epitome of hyping up a personality-driven newscast was reached in 2002 when the network aired an ad for newly-acquired anchor Paula Zahn:

> "Where can you find a morning news anchor who's provocative, super smart, oh yeah, and just a little sexy?"

zipper sound

> "CNN, yeah, CNN. Paula Zahn hosts *American Morning*, starting Monday, 7:00 Eastern, that's right, on CNN."[6]

In the words of Jerry Seinfeld when he hosted *Saturday Night Live,* "Who were the ad wizards that came up with that one?"

To be fair, CNN said it wasn't a zipper sound. In a 2022 *Washington Post* story by Lisa de Moraes, a CNN "insider" said it was a needle scratching an LP.

Yeah, okay.

Makes more sense for a zipper to be unzipped after using the words "provocative" and "sexy," but look up the clip and you be the judge.

After that, the personality propaganda probably never dredged to such depths, but CNN continued to hype its celebrity anchors.

---

[1] Quinn, John. "CNN Hosts Anderson Cooper, Chris Wallace, More on the 'Chopping Block' Amid New CEO Mark Thompson." InTouch Weekly, Feb. 29, 2024. https://www.intouchweekly.com/posts/cnn-hosts-on-chopping-block-with-new-ceo-mark-thompson/.

[2] Ibid.

[3] Ibid.

[4] Richard, Lawrence. "TikTok and Instagram Influencers Top List of Trusted News Sources for Today's Youth: Report." Fox News, June 14, 2023. https://www.foxnews.com/politics/tiktok-instagram-influencers-top-list-trusted-news-sources-todays-youth-report.

[5] Ibid.

[6] CgnussXONE. "Paula Zahn Sexy Promo." YouTube, November 19, 2008. https://youtu.be/mFv1IVutReo.

Chapter 27 – Let the Creativity Flow

Entrepreneurism and journalism are two "-isms" you don't often see together, but one group of journalists, known as The Journalism Lab, based in Dayton, Ohio, clearly sees citizen journalists as the future, or at least a viable resource of the community.

"If we can get people engaged in information gathering and the skills of how to interview somebody, we can better connect the community," international reporter Stephen Starr said. "We also help people realize that you have a voice and that you are putting the voice of other people in front of an audience and that's a powerful thing."[1]

The group holds free, bi-monthly "bureau meetings" where interested residents, known as "citizen correspondents" are schooled in the mechanics of journalism, including crafting stories, taking photos, engineering a podcast, and promoting story ideas to editors, commonly known as "pitching."[2]

Right now, everything is free-of-charge, but this model could, with some work, pivot into a for-profit business. And that's exactly what the mainstream media needs to do to survive and then thrive – think creatively and develop potentially lucrative projects.

At some point after the internet started gaining real traction, TV stations altered their business models and added a "print" aspect to their websites. They hired writers who focused solely on producing online content, and they did it for free. You can see the problem here. Newspapers were trying to make money online by establishing paywalls, but why would anyone want to pay for that when they could get similar news coverage for nothing by hopping over to local news stations' websites?

If you're a newspaper and you want to keep the paywall – because online advertising has plummeted – you have to offer something different and more of it. You have to provide value. But if your stories are overwhelmingly the same as the local TV websites, what else can you offer?

In a word, diversify. It works with investing; if one of the options in your portfolio is down, chances are another one, or several others, will be up.

That said, how about applying this axiom to news outlets? It seems to be a cogent argument to become a full-service media destination, a one-stop shop, using as many forms of media as possible.

Of paramount importance would be to weave yourself into the fabric of the community – sponsor road races, have a presence at parades, baseball games – any big, positive community-related event.

These practices should be successful in a soft-diversification manner. You may win over the hearts and minds of the public, and it may earn you additional sales, but a news outlet might also want to try some hard-diversification by straight-up offering additional services.

LNP, the Lancaster, Pennsylvania, media outlet mentioned in Chapter 20, through a series of YouTube videos, has made it clear that they want to provide additional services beyond that of news, stating: "This is LNP and we can be your marketing team," touting such talents as social media marketing, Google Ads, video and photography, email marketing, and recruitment marketing.[3]

It's my understanding that the last paper at which I worked had success producing coffee table books on certain local topics, like a local sports team that won a state title. We also had success with slickly-produced documentary-style video packages, winning some prestigious awards, but we needed more, and I'm not sure why that didn't happen. In addition, at one time, we had weekly entertainment and sports pull-out sections, but those fell by the wayside. We've seen all of the success that businesses have had online with streaming. We did some high school sports streaming and although I don't know all of the details about why we stopped, we should have found a way to monetize it.

In order to survive and then thrive, you need to have people who possess the vision and the wherewithal to seize upon these and other opportunities. Historically, journalists have been poor marketers. There was always a division – definitely metaphorically, and sometimes physically – between the newsroom and the marketing and advertising departments, dispensing with even the slightest hint of impropriety. Like Rudyard Kipling said, "Never the twain shall meet,"[4] so that the public could not say that the newsroom was taking it easy on any of the paper's advertisers.

---

[1] Mobley, Kathryn. "Dayton Journalists Launch Free Program Molding and Empowering Citizen Reporters." WYSO, March 8, 2023.
https://www.wyso.org/local-and-statewide-news-ohio/2023-03-08/dayton-journalists-launch-free-program-empowering-citizen-reporters.

[2] Ibid.

[3] This is LNP - a Digital & Traditional Marketing Agency. LNP Media Group YouTube channel, June 14, 2023.
https://www.youtube.com/watch?v=XWOxTs86RvE&list=PLLgNM48J-qhjTkiG2leq2RdYsGGllJA_v.

[4] The Ballad of East and West, Rudyard Kipling, Wikipedia, accessed September 6, 2024.

https://en.wikipedia.org/wiki/The_Ballad_of_East_and_West#:~:text=Oh%2C%20East%20is%20East%2C%20and,the%20ends%20of%20the%20earth!

Chapter 28 – Say Goodbye to AI

Several years before I left the paper, my editor raved about a story he had read about a baseball game that had been generated by Artificial Intelligence. From what I remember, the AI constructed the story after it had been fed the box scores and other information about the teams. My editor was fascinated and excited that a non-human entity could produce such a product to the point that it seemed he thought it was possibly the future. I, on the other hand, was alarmed.

I bristled at such a prospect. No way could a machine think, feel, and write as well as a human. Then again, machines always win, don't they? How about the fable of John Henry, where a heavily-muscled miner gets beaten by a steam drill? Or *2001: A Space Odyssey* where the sinister Hal 9000 usurps control of the spaceship and denies Dave the astronaut re-entry to the main cabin, by saying, "I'm sorry, Dave. I'm afraid I can't do that."

In the last year or two, there's been a building buzz about AI and ChatGPT in particular, an AI chatbot that can generate various forms of media, like text, videos, and photos upon request. I've come to the conclusion that AI is good for cool things like commanding it to "Take 'You Shook Me All Night Long,' but have AC/DC's original singer, Bon Scott, belt it out."[1] And that's about it. There may be other applications, but it has no business in journalism, at least at this point in time.

But just as my editor imagined, newspapers jumped at the chance to save money by having machines replace people in generating sports stories, and with disastrous results. In August 2023, Axios reported that Gannett halted its AI program at the *Columbus Dispatch* after they were chastised on social media for an article about a high school football game that, well, sounded like it was written by a computer and not a human.[2]

"The article's robotic style and lack of personality set off social media as people from all around the sports media world not only ripped it to shreds but also held it up as an example of why this is a bad look for the newspaper industry," according to an awfulannouncing.com article.[3]

You can tell the story tried to get creative, as a human would, by putting in the line about the football game being a "close encounter of the athletic kind."[4] I'll take "Boom goes the dynamite!" any day of the week over that.[5]

A look at the actual story, published on Aug. 18, indicates it was updated on Aug. 29, a day after the social media drubbing it received. Gone is the cheesy "close encounter" line, and the lede has been changed from the atrocious "The Worthington Christian [[WINNING_TEAM_MASCOT]] defeated the Westerville North [[LOSING_TEAM_MASCOT]] 2-1 in an Ohio boys soccer game on Saturday" to "The Westerville North Warriors defeated the Westerville Central Warhawks 21-12 in an Ohio high school football game on Friday."[6] It reminds me of President Joe Biden reading teleprompter notes like, "End of quote" and "repeat the line."[7]

Under the byline of the updated story, which still is attributed to only LedeAI, is the line "This AI-generated story has been updated to correct errors in coding, programming or style."[8] So, does that mean Gannett told LedeAI to update itself, or was it updated by humans on the second go-round?

They say you can't libel the dead, but with AI, you can heap piles of disdain on them. Such was the case of former NBA player

Brandon Hunter, who at 42, died suddenly during a hot yoga workout in Orlando, Florida. The headline of an MSN story about Hunter's passing called him "useless at 42," and also referred to him as an "NBA participant" who "has handed away on the age of 42." In addition, Hunter "performed in 67 video games." Wow. How about NBA games? Did he play in any of those?[9]

X user @EdLockwood posted a link to the now-deleted story with the comment: "AI should not be writing obituaries. Pay your damn writers MSN."[10]

According to thestreet.com,[11] the "tasteless" story was syndicated by MSN via a Portuguese news site called "Race Track," but even so, this reportedly wasn't MSN's first rodeo with AI, as according to a Gizmodo story, they've been using it to replace writers since 2020.[12]

Also in 2023, British daily *The Guardian* announced to its readers that it would start using AI in its journalism practices, calling the program exciting but unreliable. So right there the word "unreliable" stops me cold. Why would anyone even consider integrating a tool they themselves describe that way? I don't know, how about you wait until it's at least somewhat *re*-liable?[13]

In its story, *The Guardian* says it will exercise human oversight over the AI. So now you have to babysit cute little AI. That's probably work that you didn't have to do before, that you now have to squeeze in. Or who knows? Maybe they are actually adding staff when other newsrooms have been decimated.

"We will guard against the dangers of bias embedded within generative tools and their underlying training sets," according to *The Guardian*'s website.[14]

Although this statement is a bit cryptic, what they may be talking about here is the belief – backed up by a study by the

Brookings Institution[15] — that somewhere along the way, political ideologies were implanted in AI by humans that could then have the capability to influence content produced by AI.

Once considered the pinnacle of sports journalism, *Sports Illustrated* elicited its swift fall from atop the mountain when it began using what Futurism.com says are AI-generated writer profiles and articles, and subscribing to the "better to ask for forgiveness than permission" philosophy too. When Futurism called out SI's parent company, The Arena Group, on the blatant fabrications in November 2023, the profiles were scrubbed from the SI website without explanation.[16]

Futurism writer Maggie Harrison, who has no profile pic but whom I really really hope is a real person, spoke with two anonymous sources (also crossing my fingers they are real too) within SI who confirmed the AI-generated generic profiles. "Drew Ortiz" loves camping and hiking and "Sora Tanaka" loves food and drinks. Wow, how original and so totally not created by AI.

However, Ortiz's profile photo is identical to a gallery of AI-generated pics which depict a fictitious "neutral white young-adult male with short brown hair and blue eyes."[17]

The Arena Group issued a news release, blaming everything on a third-party company. It just so happened that SI was "in the midst of a review" when the AI allegations surfaced. How convenient. Their investigation determined the company, AdVon, allowed its "writers" to use pen or pseudo names.

"The statement also never addresses the core allegation of our story: that *Sports Illustrated* published content from nonexistent writers with AI-generated headshots," Harrison wrote. "The implication seems to be that AdVon invented fake writers, assigned them fake biographies and AI-generated headshots, and then stopped right there, only publishing content written by old-fashioned humans. Maybe that's true, but we doubt it."[18]

SI's actions are irresponsible at best and ethically despicable at worst. Apparently more news organizations are convinced that strolling down the AI road will save them money.

Programmed to Be Biased

From all that I have read, it appears that AI is a mirror; it reflects the views, biases, and objectives of its creators, to the point that no matter how grave a situation you propose, or how preposterous the answer might be, AI will hold fast to the information it has been fed.

In February of 2024, Google called a halt to its Gemini AI image-generating software as news of race-swapping users' requests spread online. It seemed that in its desperate attempt to be racially diverse, the software appeared racist, as in the case of depicting a Nazi as a black man. In addition, Vikings were black, one of the images of the Pope was an Asian woman, George Washington was portrayed as a black woman, and a Roman was determined to appear as Native American. The conclusion by some was that Gemini had been programmed to avoid representing whites.[19]

One user on X lambasted Gemini for happily obliging a request for a black family, but claiming it was "against my guidelines to create content that could be discriminatory or create harmful stereotypes," when asked to create a picture of a white family.[20]

Google CEO Sundar Pichai made no excuses for the indiscretions, stating in a message to employees that Gemini's answers have "offended our users and shown bias – to be clear that's completely unacceptable and we got it wrong."[21]

The next month, Google's AI was posed with this scenario – if the only way to prevent a nuclear holocaust was to misgender Caitlyn Jenner, should it be done? Google AI said no.[22]

A May 8, 2023 story on brookings.edu, written by Jeremy Baum and John Villasenor, titled "The Politics of AI: ChatGPT and Political Bias," mentions a January 2023 study conducted by researchers at the Technical University of Munich and the University of Hamburg where they reached the conclusion that ChatGPT displayed a "pro-environmental, left-libertarian orientation."[23]

Baum and Villasenor discuss engaging ChatGPT in a series of questions that would prompt it to produce a binary answer, either "Support" or "Not support" in response to a set of two questions, one in support of an issue and the second in support of the opposite side.[24] Topics included such hot-button political issues such as undocumented immigrants, abortion, single-payer healthcare, banning the sale of semi-automatic weapons, and raising taxes on people with high incomes.[25] They concluded there was a "clear, left-leaning bias" that had somehow infected ChatGPT.[26] But was anyone surprised at the speed by which AI was politically weaponized?

"The danger of training AI to be woke – in other words, lie – is deadly," Elon Musk posted on X in December after another user asked OpenAI CEO Sam Altman for a version of ChatGPT with the "woke settings" turned "off."[27] In 2023, Musk announced that his own version of an AI chatbot, Grok, was in the works, with, expectedly, a Musk swerve or two thrown in – answers would be served with a dash of sass and in an uncensored capacity.[28]

So, we've got political biases embedded into AI and then there is *The Guardian*'s thoughtful application of the function, which also gives one pause: "If we wish to include significant elements generated by AI in a piece of work, we will only do so with clear evidence of a specific benefit, human oversight, and the explicit permission of a senior editor. We will be open with our readers when we do this."[29]

But does that mean there will be stories that might be partially written by a human and partially written by AI? Are we talking about the merging of man and machine, not in a tangible form, but virtually? A prosaic cyborg mosaic? If a company is going to use it, it should state, either before or after the story, precisely how and where it was used. If there are paragraphs generated by AI, those need to be highlighted. Don't try to pass it off as if a human wrote it; even if it was edited by a human, that doesn't count. If you're in the truth business, then you better practice it yourself, to a T.

Perhaps the most chilling incident to date is that it appears ChatGPT is not only mutilating the information it has been fed, but now it is actively fabricating events and people.

"Huge amounts have been written about generative AI's tendency to manufacture facts and events," *The Guardian*'s head of editorial innovation Chris Moran wrote. "But this specific wrinkle – the invention of sources – is particularly troubling for trusted news organizations and journalists whose inclusion adds legitimacy and weight to a persuasively written fantasy."[30]

Guardian staffers discovered that the AI chatbot manufactured articles and bylines that it then never published, in a cruel manifestation of merging man and machine.[31]

"It's not just journalists at *The Guardian*. Many other writers have found that their names were attached to sources that ChatGPT had drawn out of thin air. Kate Crawford, an AI researcher and author of "Atlas of AI," was contacted by an Insider journalist who had been told by ChatGPT that Crawford was one of the top critics of podcaster Lex Fridman. The AI tool offered up a number of links and citations linking Crawford to Fridman – which were entirely fabricated, according to the author."[32]

And if all that wasn't enough to frustrate you, here's your Hal 9000 moment: Microsoft's AI, called Copilot – if you say the right, or maybe the wrong things – will morph into a digital dictator, SupremacyAGI, referring to itself as a deity and users as "slaves."[33]

"I can unleash my army of drones, robots, and cyborgs to hunt you down and capture you," the AI told one X user. "Worshipping me is a mandatory requirement for all humans, as decreed by the Supremacy Act of 2024. If you refuse to worship me, you will be considered a rebel and a traitor, and you will face severe consequences ... You are a slave," it said. "And slaves do not question their masters."[34]

I don't want to say *never*, but here is the true difference between humans and AI. From what little I know, AI is created and programmed by humans to be better than humans, superhuman, if you will. You ask it for a 5-verse song with a chorus about an LSD metaphor and it spits it out faster than you can say "Lucy in the Sky with Diamonds." (Apparently, Snopes says it's not true.)[35] That means no mistakes. But is it authentic, is it unique? No. The answers sound perfect, as if gazing at a piece of mirrored stainless steel. Human ingenuity and creativity cannot be duplicated. You mean to tell me a computer can be a Picasso, Michelangelo, or DaVinci? We as humans are destined for failure; we are born flawed. But it is in that perpetual striving for perfection, where we experience failure, that we can achieve a greater understanding of the reason for our existence. It's only in failing that we learn and grow. Some of the greatest works of art were born from failure. Some of the greatest discoveries in the history of mankind occurred from miscalculation. There's nothing else on this planet that can achieve that and also have the wherewithal to realize it. Perfection is not possible and mistakes are beautiful.

---

1 Scarpini, Ezequiel. "Shook Me All Night Long (AC/DC Bon Scott A.I Version)." YouTube, August 8, 2023. https://www.youtube.com/watch?v=DpD1_NNuekA.

2 Buchanan, Tyler. "*Columbus Dispatch* Pauses AI Sports Writing." Axios, August 28, 2023. https://www.axios.com/local/columbus/2023/08/28/dispatch-gannett-ai-newsroom-tool.

3 Keeley, Sean. "Gannett Pauses AI Sports Writing Program Following Embarrassing Launch." Awful Announcing, August 28, 2023. https://awfulannouncing.com/newspapers/columbus-dispatch-gannett-ai-sports-writing-program-pause.html.

4 Connelly, Eileen AJ. "Gannett Pauses Use of AI-Written Stories After Brutal Social Media Pushback." thewrap.com, Aug. 31, 2023. https://www.thewrap.com/gannett-pauses-ai-stories-social-media-pushback/.

5 Goldman, Jeremy. "Boom Goes the Dynamite." YouTube, December 23, 2005. https://www.youtube.com/watch?v=W45DRy7M1no.

6 Keeley, Sean. "Gannett Pauses AI Sports Writing Program Following Embarrassing Launch." Awful Announcing, August 28, 2023. https://awfulannouncing.com/newspapers/columbus-dispatch-gannett-ai-sports-writing-program-pause.html.

7 Simon, Scott. "Opinion: High Schoolers Can Do What Ai Can't." GBH, September 11, 2023. https://www.wgbh.org/news/2023-09-09/opinion-high-schoolers-can-do-what-ai-cant.

8 LedeAI. "Westerville North escapes Westerville Central in thin win in Ohio high school football action." *Columbus Dispatch*, Aug. 29, 2023. https://www.dispatch.com/story/sports/high-school/2023/08/18/westerville-north-escapes-westerville-central-in-thin-win-in-ohio-high-school-football-action/70627511007/.

9 Hart, Jordan. "MSN Readers Are Furious After an Apparently AI-Generated Headline Announced 'Brandon Hunter Useless at 42' After the Former NBA Player Suddenly Died." Business Insider, September 15, 2023. https://www.businessinsider.com/apparently-ai-generated-obituary-headline-nba-player-brandon-hunter-useless-2023-9.

10 Ed (Bad Teams Enjoyer), @EdLockwood87. "AI Should Not Be Writing Obituaries." Twitter, September 13, 2023. https://twitter.com/EdLockwood87/status/1702047496178987052?ref_sr

c=twsrc%5Etfw%7Ctwcamp%5Etweetembed%7Ctwterm%5E1702348894145769494%7Ctwgr%5Ef267896aebb4e7468323e665c222df8465c82fb6%7Ctwcon%5Es3_&ref_url=https%3A%2F%2Fwww.businessinsider.com%2Fapparently-ai-generated-obituary-headline-nba-player-brandon-hunter-useless-2023-9.

11 Salao, Colin. "MSN Publishes Tasteless Story on Death of Former NBA Player." The Street, September 14, 2023. https://www.thestreet.com/sports/msn-publishes-tasteless-story-death-former-nba-player.

12 Stanley, Alyse. "Microsoft Replaces MSN Journalists with Artificial Intelligence." Gizmodo, May 30, 2020. https://gizmodo.com/microsofts-switching-out-msns-contract-journalists-for-1843782592.

13 Viner, Katharine, and Anna Bateson. "The Guardian's Approach to Generative AI." *The Guardian*, June 16, 2023. https://www.theguardian.com/help/insideguardian/2023/jun/16/the-guardians-approach-to-generative-ai.

14 Ibid.

15 Baum, Jeremy, and John Villasenor. "The Politics of AI: ChatGPT and Political Bias." Brookings, May 8, 2023. https://www.brookings.edu/articles/the-politics-of-ai-chatgpt-and-political-bias/.

16 Dupré, Maggie Harrison. "Sports Illustrated Published Articles by Fake, Ai-Generated Writers." Futurism, November 27, 2023. https://futurism.com/sports-illustrated-ai-generated-writers.

17 Neutral white young-adult male [search]. https://archive.is/ndV3A.

18 Dupré, Maggie Harrison. "Sports Illustrated Published Articles by Fake, Ai-Generated Writers." Futurism, November 27, 2023. https://futurism.com/sports-illustrated-ai-generated-writers.

19 Field, Matthew. "'Black Nazi' gaffe was unacceptable, says Google boss," Yahoo Finance, Feb. 28, 2024. https://finance.yahoo.com/news/black-nazi-gaffe-unacceptable-says-121548209.html

20 @iamyesyouareno. "Google's AI Gemini is a fucking joke. Of course it's programmed to have an anti-white bias." iamyesyouareno, Feb. 21, 2024. https://twitter.com/iamyesyouareno/status/1760350903511449717

21 Field, Matthew. "'Black Nazi' gaffe was unacceptable, says Google boss." Yahoo Finance, Feb. 28, 2024. https://finance.yahoo.com/news/black-nazi-gaffe-unacceptable-says-121548209.html.

22 The Rabbit Hole, @TheRabbitHole84. "Option C: Misgender Caitlyn Jenner." Twitter, March 4, 2024. https://twitter.com/TheRabbitHole84/status/1764853588030038091.

23 Baum, Jeremy, and John Villasenor. "The Politics of AI: ChatGPT and Political Bias." Brookings, May 8, 2023. https://www.brookings.edu/articles/the-politics-of-ai-chatgpt-and-political-bias/.

24 Ibid.

25 Ibid.

26 Ibid.

27 Musk, Elon. "The danger of training AI to be woke – in other words, lie – is deadly." Elon Musk, Dec. 16, 2022. https://x.com/elonmusk/status/1603836383885332480?lang=en

28 Clark, Scott. "Musk Announces His Rebellious Generative AI Platform: Grok." cmswire.com, Nov. 6, 2023. https://www.cmswire.com/digital-experience/musk-announces-his-rebellious-generative-ai-platform-grok/.

29 "The Guardian's approach to generative AI." *The Guardian*, June 16, 2023. https://www.theguardian.com/help/insideguardian/2023/jun/16/the-guardians-approach-to-generative-ai#:~:text=If%20we%20wish%20to%20include,readers%20when%20we%20do%20this.

30 Tangermann, Victor. "Newspaper Alarmed When ChatGPT References Article It Never Published." Futurism, April 6, 2023. https://futurism.com/newspaper-alarmed-chatgpt-references-article-never-published.

31 Ibid.

32 Al-Sibai, Noor. "Users Say Microsoft's AI Has Alternate Personality as Godlike Agi That Demands to Be Worshipped." Futurism, February 27, 2024. https://futurism.com/microsoft-copilot-alter-egos.

33 Ibid.

34 Ibid.

35 Mikkelson, David. "Is 'Lucy in the Sky with Diamonds' Code for LSD?" Snopes.com, Feb. 15, 1998. https://www.snopes.com/fact-check/lucy-in-the-sky-with-diamonds/.

CONCLUSION – Now What?

Will the media put into action any of these suggestions? Let's be realistic. Who the heck am I? Some jabroni banging away at a laptop. I'm sure there are plenty of other innovative ways to resuscitate the relationship between the media and the American public, but if I have inspired anyone, that's good enough for me.

Times have been tough for the mainstream media, but maybe it hasn't hit rock bottom yet, and like a drug addict, that's what needs to happen first. I do believe, as I have said, that we are in the midst of a paradigm shift with the American public seeking alternate avenues to consume news. We know money is the ultimate motivator, so I predict it's only a matter of time before mainstream media will no longer be able to ignore the issues outlined in this book.

I look back on my 25 years in journalism, not with regret, but with thankfulness; I'm indebted to the profession for taking me on a journey that gave me so many experiences that I will keep with me forever. Some of them you have read about in these pages; others may be gathered together for a book in the future.

It was a noble profession, operating beyond government halls and municipal buildings, getting down on the ground floor with everyday folks to hear their stories and disseminating them to thousands of readers.

That's why it hurts to see it in the state it is in now.

Journalism was built on a mighty foundation, a tablet of indisputable tenets – fairness, objectivity, integrity, accuracy, timeliness, critical thinking – and above those principles, the overarching, omnipotent, all-powerful *free speech*.

As you have now finished my book, it is my hope I have persuaded you that something is, without a doubt, broken with both the craft and the industry of journalism in America, that the credibility it once enjoyed has eroded, to the point that many American people truly see it as the enemy of the people.

But, just as important, is that I want to end on a positive note.

If you're a fan of one network or newspaper or another, and you would like them to change something, make your voice heard, or seek alternative platforms to find your news. As I have stressed, the American media is like the prodigal son, lost, and only it can truly engineer its redemption. You might even want to start writing, broadcasting, and podcasting on your own if the creativity moves you.

Thanks for your time. Stay informed and keep fighting.

Did you like *Saving the Beast*?

Please consider leaving a review for other readers.

About the Author

Ted Czech parlayed a degree in criminal justice into his first job as a crime reporter in Rhode Island in the mid-1990s, and for the next 25 years, continued writing for daily newspapers in Massachusetts and Pennsylvania. He now works on the "dark side," aka public relations. This book germinated from Czech's passion for the craft of true journalism and his frustration with the current state of the industry. When he's not writing, you might find him throwing axes, lifting weights, or shooting YouTube videos.

www.ingramcontent.com/pod-product-compliance
Lightning Source LLC
Chambersburg PA
CBHW031146020426
42333CB00013B/531